Napoleon Hill

How to Create a

MOTIVATED MINDSET

Napoleon Hill's

How to Create a

MOTIVATED
MINDSET

NAPOLEON HILL FOUNDATION

Published and distributed by:
SOUND WISDOM
P.O. Box 310
Shippensburg, PA 17257-0310
717-530-2122

info@soundwisdom.com

www.soundwisdom.com

While efforts have been made to verify information contained in this publication, neither the author nor the publisher assumes any responsibility for errors, inaccuracies, or omissions. While this publication is chock-full of useful, practical information; it is not intended to be legal or accounting advice. All readers are advised to seek competent lawyers and accountants to follow laws and regulations that may apply to specific situations. The reader of this publication assumes responsibility for the use of the information. The author and publisher assume no responsibility or liability whatsoever on the behalf of the reader of this publication.

ISBN 13 TP: 978-1-64095-461-8

ISBN 13 eBook: 978-1-64095-462-5

For Worldwide Distribution, Printed in the U.S.A.

1 2 3 4 5 6 7 8 / 28 27 26 25 24

CONTENTS

INTRODUCTION

Napoleon Hill was 69 years old and planning to retire when he honored one of his few remaining speaking commitments at a Dental Convention in Chicago in 1952. Wealthy insurance magnate W. Clement Stone, a longtime follower of Mr. Hill's philosophy, was invited to attend by his dentist, and did so happily, having believed Mr. Hill had passed on. Mr. Stone introduced himself to Mr. Hill and began a discussion that resulted in him coaxing Mr. Hill to continue spreading his success philosophy in partnership with him, through a company they created named Napoleon Hill Associates.

One of the goals of Napoleon Hill Associates was to train students to teach Mr. Hill's philosophy of success. To that end, in 1953 Mr. Hill delivered seventeen lectures to the assembled students, each one focused on one of the success principles he had discovered over the 45 years during his interviews with successful businessmen, inventors, statesmen, and scientists.

These lectures have never before been published in book form. The Trustees of the Napoleon Hill Foundation (established by

Napoleon Hill in 1962 and chaired for many years by Mr. Stone) have selected four of those lectures for this book. Each deals with the state of mind you must have to succeed in achieving your Definite Major Purpose. That state of mind is made up of *Enthusiasm,* a *Positive Mental Attitude, Faith,* and *Self-Discipline,* and becomes critically important after you have determined what your definite major purpose is in life. Taken together, these four states of mind create a motivated mindset, which adds up to the "burning desire" Mr. Hill so often states is necessary for anyone to achieve their goals.

Due to the wisdom and experience Napoleon Hill had gained over the years, the tenor of these lectures tended to be more philosophical than some of his past lectures and writings. This is evident at the outset of Chapter 1, "Enthusiasm's Positive Influence," which sets forth quotations from a number of philosophers on the subject. Mr. Hill lists the many benefits of Enthusiasm, the most important of which, he says, is that it converts negative emotions to positive ones, thus preparing the mind for the development of Faith.

Mr. Hill recounts his interviews with his mentor, Andrew Carnegie, on the subject of Enthusiasm and the benefits it brings in the workplace and the home. Mr. Carnegie identifies the major causes of the destruction of Enthusiasm, including non-constructive criticism. Mr. Hill also explains how Enthusiasm works much like prayer, and connects us to Infinite Intelligence (Mr. Hill's name for a Supreme Being). He closes with a story demonstrating how Enthusiasm can be transferred by one person to another, to the benefit of both.

The second lecture detailed in Chapter 3 deals with the principle of a Positive Mental Attitude (PMA), and is a combination of philosophical observations and practical "how to" advice. It begins with a description of the "two sealed envelopes" we are all born with, one containing *rewards* that can only be obtained by one having PMA, and the other containing the *penalties* people will endure without PMA. Mr. Hill provides a comprehensive list of steps we can take to develop PMA. This list is enlightening, and goes beyond developing PMA to detail how we can achieve our ultimate objective.

In Chapter 4 Mr. Hill explains the difference between mere wishing and believing, and sets forth how to use PMA to reach the "belief" level, which is necessary to achieve success. This is another "how to" session, and it deserves re-reading because of the many valuable tips provided. Another list is then presented, about how to achieve peace of mind, something Mr. Hill became increasingly interested in with advancing age. The list is nothing short of a blueprint for happiness. This lecture concludes with illustrations of how friends and students of Mr. Hill have used PMA to accomplish goals that others might think impossible to achieve.

Chapter 5 focuses on our need to have Faith to achieve our Major Definite Purpose. Mr. Hill does not advocate any particular religious denomination, but he does believe that a higher power, which he calls Infinite Intelligence, exists and is responsible for a person's success. He speaks eloquently about how nature and order in the world prove the existence of Infinite Intelligence.

He states that Faith is necessary to connect the mind to Infinite Intelligence. Once the connection is made, the subconscious mind takes control and leads us to achieve our Definite Major Purpose, which is the beginning of all achievement when related to a strongly compelling motive creating a state of mind necessary to take action to achieve each of your goals in life. Seven specific factors useful to help define your Definite Major Purpose are found in Napoleon Hill's book titled *Guide to Achieving Your Goals.*

To have Faith, we must rid the mind of all negative thoughts and fears, arrive at a Definite Major Purpose and a motive for achieving it, then create a plan and act upon it. In Chapter 6, Mr. Hill discusses the *seven major fears* that must be banished from the mind:

1. Poverty

2. Criticism

3. Ill health

4. Loss of love

5. Old age

6. Loss of liberty

7. Death

He describes in detail how these fears can be overcome. He discusses the need for a Positive Mental Attitude in order to develop Faith, and gives a ten-point plan for achieving PMA. Once again, Mr. Hill combines the philosophical with practical advice, demonstrating how essential Faith is as part of our state of mind to achieve our goals.

In Chapter 7, you will learn how to attract the vitalizing influence of Infinite Intelligence and focus it on the object of desire. You will have the whole process laid before you, realizing it is a process going on all around you, in countless forms of life. It is not a matter of theory, it is a demonstrated fact. You have only to adapt it to your purpose.

The last two chapters in this book deal with a principle Mr. Hill often refers to as the most essential key to controlling our mind, Self-Discipline, which deals with a state of mind we must have to create the *burning desire* needed to achieve a Definite Major Purpose.

An insightful presentation is shared of Self-Discipline's ten benefits, all of which Mr. Hill promises his students they will enjoy if they gain control over their minds. He offers many definitions and explanations of this state of mind such as taking possession of your mind, mastering your thoughts, thinking before acting, controlling emotions, controlling thought habits, and belief in yourself. He lists the fourteen major emotions and explains how they must be controlled by Self-Discipline if you are to succeed. Regarding control of thought habits, he expounds on how the mind and the heart, reason and emotion, must be kept in balance by Self-Discipline.

He then explains how Self-Discipline is also essential for controlling our mental attitude, budgeting time, and concentrating on Definiteness of Purpose. Mr. Hill recounts the methods and achievements of people who used Self-Discipline to achieve their goals. They include freedom activist Mahatma Gandhi, an immigrant fruit peddler who founded the Bank of America, and Napoleon Hill himself.

The final chapter concludes with a mixture of science and philosophy, in which Mr. Hill describes the divisions of the mind, six of which can be controlled by Self-Discipline. After reading this concluding chapter, we think you will come to believe as Mr. Hill does, that Self-Discipline is indeed a most significant attribute, necessary for controlling many aspects of life, and for ultimately achieving your Definite Major Purpose.

We at the Napoleon Hill Foundation hope this book—concentrating on the emotions and states of mind that can be controlled, motivated, and used to create the burning desire you need to achieve happiness and success—will be of great benefit to you.

Don M. Green
Chief Executive Officer and Executive Director
Napoleon Hill Foundation

1

ENTHUSIASM'S POSITIVE INFLUENCE

English writer Henry Chester gave a marvelous dissertation on enthusiasm when he said:

Enthusiasm is one of the greatest assets of man. It beats money and power and influence. Single handed the enthusiast convinces and dominates where the wealth accumulated by a small army of workers would scarcely raise a tremor of interest. Enthusiasm tramples over prejudice and opposition, spurns inaction, storms the citadel of its object and, like an avalanche, overwhelms and engulfs all obstacles. It is nothing less nor more than faith in action.

Faith and initiative rightly combined remove mountainous barriers and achieve the unheard of and miraculous. Set the germ of enthusiasm afloat in your plant, in your office, or on your farm; carry it in your attitude and manner; it spreads and influences every fiber of your industry before you realize it; it means increase in production and decrease in costs; it means joy and pleasure, and satisfaction to your workers; it means life, real, virile; it means spontaneous, rock-bed results–the vital things that pay big dividends–throughout life.

Yes, enthusiasm bears the same relationship to a human being that fire bears to a steam boiler. It concentrates the powers of the mind and gives them the wings of action.

Enthusiasm is the offspring of motive!

Every philosopher and every thinker has discovered that enthusiasm gives added meaning to words and changes the meaning of deeds, and some have discovered that it gives greater power to thought, as well as to the spoken word. Enthusiasm is the offspring of motive!

Give a man a burning desire to achieve a definite end, and a definite motive back of that desire, and lo! the flame of enthusiasm begins to burn within him, and appropriate action follows immediately.

American essayist and philosopher Ralph Waldo Emerson said:

> I have heard an experienced counsellor say that he feared never the effect upon a jury of a lawyer who does not believe in his heart that his client ought to win a verdict. If he does not believe it, his unbelief will appear to the jury, despite all his protestations, and will become their unbelief. This is the law whereby a work of art, of whatsoever kind, sets us in the same state of mind wherein the artist was when he made it. That which we do not believe, we cannot adequately say, though we may repeat the words ever so often.

Emerson has stated a fact that is known to all who observe closely, but he has not explained the cause behind it. How and why does a jury pick up the unbelief of a lawyer when it is the direct opposite of his spoken words? Why are the words ignored while something stronger than words reaches and influences the minds of the jury? What is this "something," and what causes it to function?

Prolific inventor Dr. Elmer R. Gates gave the answer to these questions more than 30 years ago, when he demonstrated that every brain is both a broadcasting station and a receiving station for the vibrations of thought, that highly emotionalized thought (enthusiasm is intense emotion) penetrates the minds of all within access of its range, and in this manner we reveal the true nature of our thoughts, even though they may not harmonize with our spoken words.

Orison Swett Marden, writer and founder of *SUCCESS* magazine, said:

> The faculty to dream was not given to mock us. There is a reality back of it. There is a divinity behind our legitimate desires. By the desires that have divinity in them, we do not refer to the things that we want but do not need; we do not refer to the desires that turn to Dead Sea fruit on our lips, or to ashes when eaten, but to the legitimate desires of the soul for the realization of those ideals, the longing for full, complete self-expression, the time and opportunity for the weaving of the pattern shown in the moment of our highest transfiguration.

Dr. Marden might well have said "in the moment of our highest enthusiasm," for that was what he meant. "Our mental attitude, our heart's desire," he explained, "is our perpetual prayer which Nature answers. She takes it for granted that we desire what we are headed toward, and she helps us to it." He might have expressed it, "She takes for granted we desire what we are most enthusiastic about."

Dr. Marden added, "People little realize that their desires are their perpetual prayers–not head prayers, but heart prayers–and that they are always granted. Most people do not half realize how sacred a thing legitimate ambition is. What is this eternal urge within us which is trying to push us on, up and up? It is the urge (enthusiasm), the push in the great force within us, which is perpetually prodding us to do our best and refuses to accept our second best."

Yes, Dr. Marden was speaking of enthusiasm when he referred to "the great force within us which is perpetually prodding us to do our best." He was speaking of that intense feeling of emotion known as a burning desire, without which words fail to carry conviction, deeds fail to impress, and actions fall short of their intended mark.

Without a burning desire, words carry no conviction, deeds fail to impress, and actions fall short.

A writer who covered women's roles in the advancement of society, Lillian Whiting had caught the spirit and the meaning of enthusiasm when she stated, "No one has success until he has the abounding life. This is made up of many-fold activity of energy, enthusiasm and gladness. It is to spring to meet the day with the thrill of being alive. It is to go forth to meet the morning in an ecstasy of joy. It is to realize the oneness of humanity in true spiritual sympathy."

Philip James Bailey, English poet, understood the power of enthusiasm when he wrote:

> We live in deeds, not years; in thoughts, not breaths;
> In feelings, not in figures on a dial.
> We should count time by heart throbs.
> He most lives
> Who thinks most, feels noblest, acts the best.

Yes, that is true, and one "feels the noblest, acts the best" when the inspiration of enthusiasm drives him onward toward the attainment of some pre-established goal.

Influential English intellectual Leigh Hunt understood the meaning of enthusiasm when he asserted: "There are two worlds: the world that we can measure with line and rule, and the world that we feel with our hearts and imagination."

Johann Fitche, German philosopher, disclosed his deep understanding of the power of enthusiasm in these words:

> My philosophy makes life—the system of feelings and desires—supreme, and leaves knowledge merely the post of observer. This system of feelings is a fact in our minds about which there can be no dispute, and a fact of which we have intuitive knowledge, a knowledge not inferred by arguments, nor generated

by reasoning which can be received or neglected as we choose. Only such face-to-face knowledge has reality. It alone can get life into motion, since it springs from life.

Ancient Roman dramatist Terence recognized the power of enthusiasm in the statement, "You believe that easily which you hope for earnestly." And former U.S. President James A. Garfield expressed the same thought in these words: "If wrinkles must be written upon our brows, let them be not written upon the heart. The spirit should not grow old." He understood that the heart is the seat of enthusiasm, the source of all emotional feeling, the mainstay of all individual power of expression.

Enthusiasm's power transmutes adversities, failures, and temporary defeat into action-backed faith.

Enthusiasm is a power by which adversities and failures and temporary defeat may be transmuted into action-backed faith. This is perhaps the most impressive single truth that has been presented through the philosophy of individual achievement, for it can be nothing less than profoundly impressive for a person to realize that sorrow and adversity can be transmuted into an impelling enthusiasm of sufficient force to enable people to surmount all difficulties.

Those who are informed in metaphysics know that material circumstances mean nothing to the person who understands how to turn on this enthusiasm at will, that material circumstances shape themselves to fit the state of their mind as naturally as water runs downhill in response to the law of gravitation.

The metaphysician knows that the death of a dear friend or loved one need not merely bring sorrow, but it may serve as an inspiration to nobler efforts and deeper thinking, through the principle of transmutation of emotional feeling.

The power of thought is the one unsolved mystery of the world!

Thought is an expression of energy, and it is precisely as powerful when expressed in a negative form as it is when it is expressed in a positive form. The energy of thought, therefore, used to express the feeling of great sorrow, or loss, or disappointment, can be transmuted into positive expression and made to serve as an inspiration to noble endeavor.

The transmutation hinges entirely upon the control of the emotions, hence the necessity of acquiring the habit of voluntary expression of enthusiasm.

There is but one kind of thought energy, but it can be given many kinds of expression, either negative or positive, or a combination of both.

Reasoning on this simple premise, we can easily see that any negative emotion can be changed into a positive feeling that will be helpful. In this possibility, we may find the most profound application for the emotion of enthusiasm, which is vital for a motivated mindset.

Enthusiasm is the action factor of thought!

The same energy that brings the pain of sorrow may be converted and made to bring the joy of creative action in connection with our Definite Major Purpose, or some minor purpose. Here is where self-discipline comes to our aid, for only the self-disciplined person can transmute sorrow into joy.

SOME BENEFITS OF CONTROLLED ENTHUSIASM

Controlled enthusiasm:

- Steps up the power of thought and thereby makes the faculty of the imagination more alert.
- Clears the mind of negative emotions by transmuting them into positive emotions, thereby preparing the way for the expression of faith.
- Gives a pleasing, convincing "color" to the tone of the voice.
- Definitely takes the drudgery out of labor.
- Adds to the attractiveness of the personality.
- Inspires self-confidence.

When accompanied by appropriate physical action, enthusiasm:

- Becomes of major importance in transmuting negative emotion into positive emotion.

- Gives the necessary force to our desires and thereby influences the subconscious section of the mind to act with promptness on those desires.

- Generates enthusiasm on the part of others, for it is as contagious as the measles or the whooping cough.

Enthusiasm is the major factor that converts an "order taker" into a first class salesperson. And let it be remembered that there has never been a salesperson worthy of that title who could not turn on their enthusiasm at will and sustain it as long as desired.

Enthusiasm takes the "dryness" and the boredom out of public speech by establishing harmony between the speaker and the audience. Thus, it is an indispensable quality in the work of anyone whose occupation depends for its success upon the spoken word. The enthusiastic speaker takes control of the audience at will.

Enthusiasm gives brilliance to the spoken word and tends to develop an alert memory. Being a sort of radiation of spirit, enthusiasm is closely related to, or at least attuned to, Infinite Intelligence.

But far and away the most important functions of enthusiasm are these: It definitely serves as the major factor in converting negative emotion into positive emotion, and it prepares the mind for the development and expression of faith. Compared with these, all other functions of enthusiasm are inconsequential.

Enthusiasm converts negative emotion into positive emotion, preparing a motivated mindset for the development and expression of Faith.

Enthusiasm is the action factor of thought! Where it is strong enough, it literally forces you into action appropriate to the nature of the motive that inspired it.

HOW TO DEVELOP THE HABIT OF ENTHUSIASM

Accurate thinking is the "modus operandi" (MO) by which the emotions of the heart and the reasoning power of the head may be combined in whatever proportions each need may demand. Enthusiasm, therefore, is an essential factor in effective thinking.

There are certain steps to take that will lead to the development of controlled enthusiasm, including:

- Adopt a Definite Major Purpose and a definite plan for attaining it, and go to work carrying out the plan now, right where you are.

- Back that purpose with an obsessional desire (enthusiastic motive) for its attainment. Let the desire become a *burning desire!* Fan it, coax it, and let it become a dominating factor of your mind at all times. Take it to bed with you at night and get up with it in the morning. Make it the basis of all your prayers.

- Write out a clear statement of both your Definite Major Purpose and the plan by which you hope to attain it, together with a statement of what you intend to give in return for its realization.

- Follow the plan through, with persistence based on all the enthusiasm you can generate, remembering that a weak plan persistently applied is better than a strong plan applied intermittently or without enthusiasm.

- Keep as far away as possible from "joy-killers" and confirmed pessimists. Their influence is deadly. Substitute, in their place, associates who are optimistic and, above all, do not mention your plans to anyone except those who are in full sympathy with you.

- If you are overtaken by temporary defeat, study your plans carefully, and if need be, change them, but do not change your major purpose simply because you have met with temporary defeat.

- Never let a day pass without devoting some time, even though it be ever so little, to carrying out your plans. Remember, you are developing the habit of enthusiasm, and habits call for repetition through physical action.

- Auto-suggestion is a powerful factor in the development of any habit.

Therefore, keep yourself fixed on the belief that you will obtain the object of your Definite Major Purpose, no matter how far removed from you it may be. Your own mental attitude will determine the nature of the action your subconscious mind will take in connection with the fulfillment of your purpose. Keep your mind positive at all times, remembering that enthusiasm thrives only on a positive mind. It will not mix with fear, envy, greed, jealousy, doubt, revenge, hatred, intolerance and procrastination. Enthusiasm thrives on a positive action.

Enthusiasm thrives on positive action.

From here on out you are on your own! But remember that every person lives in two worlds:

1. The world of our own mental attitude, which is greatly influenced by our associates and our physical surroundings, and

2. The physical world where we must struggle for a living.

The circumstances of the physical world may be greatly shaped by the way we relate to our mental world. Our mental world we may control. The physical world is beyond our control, except to the extent that we attract that portion of it that harmonizes with our mental attitude.

Enthusiasm is a great leavening force in your mental world. Enthusiasm:

• Gives power to your purpose.

• Makes for harmony within your own mind.

• Helps to free the mind of negative influences.

• Wakes up the imagination and stirs you to action in shaping the circumstances of the physical world to your own needs.

Anyone without enthusiasm and a Definite Major Purpose resembles a locomotive with neither steam nor a track on which to run, or a destination toward which to travel. But no amount of enthusiasm can take the place of definiteness of purpose.

There are two types of enthusiasm: passive and active. Perhaps it would be more accurate to say that enthusiasm may be expressed in two ways:

1. Passively, through the stimulation of emotional feeling that inspires us to meditate and to think, in silence, and

2. Actively, by the expression of feeling, through words and deeds.

ANDREW CARNEGIE'S ANALYSIS OF ENTHUSIASM

Andrew Carnegie commissioned me to study the principles of success, and I interviewed him at length. When I asked him which of the two types of enthusiasm he regarded as the more beneficial, he said:

> That depends upon the circumstances. Passive enthusiasm always precedes the expression of active enthusiasm, through words and deeds, as one must feel enthusiasm before he can express it in any form.
>
> There are times when the expression of enthusiasm may be detrimental to one's interests, as it may indicate over-eagerness or anxiety, or disclose one's

state of mind under circumstances when he does not wish it to be known to others.

It is highly important then that one learn to withhold the expression of his feelings whenever he wills to do so. It is also important that one learn to turn on his enthusiasm and give it any desired form of expression, at will. In both instances, the control is the important thing.

The major benefits of enthusiasm are these:

- Enthusiasm stimulates the mind, and makes thought more intense; thus it starts the faculty of the imagination into operation in connection with the motive which inspired the enthusiasm.

- Enthusiasm gives tone quality to one's voice, giving it dynamic force and making it impressive. A salesman, public speaker, lawyer or clergyman would be ineffective in his speech without the ability to turn on his enthusiasm at will, and without the self-discipline to withhold it at will. Even the most prosaic subjects can be dramatized and made interesting through enthusiasm. Without it the most interesting subjects can be boring.

- Enthusiasm inspires personal initiative, both in thought and in physical action. It is very difficult for one to do his best in any kind of endeavor which does not have the support of his enthusiasm.

- Enthusiasm dispels physical fatigue and overcomes laziness. It has been said that there are no lazy men; that men who appear to be lazy are those who have not been inspired by a motive backed by enthusiasm.

- Enthusiasm stimulates the subconscious section of the brain and puts it to work in connection with the motive which inspires the enthusiasm. In fact, there is no other method of voluntarily stimulating the subconscious section of the mind except that of enthusiasm.

- Here let me emphasize the fact that the subconscious mind acts upon all emotional feeling, whether it is negative or positive. Fear, for example, is enthusiasm expressed negatively; and so are hatred and anger and jealousy and envy. It is important that one learn the difference between negative enthusiasm and positive enthusiasm, since enthusiasm is the self-starter which puts the subconscious section of the mind to work.

- Enthusiasm is more contagious than any disease. It affects everyone within its range, a fact which is well known to all master salesmen, and to all truly great leaders in every walk of life.

- Positive enthusiasm discourages all forms of negative thought, and dispels fear and worry, and thus prepares the mind for the expression of faith, which is the most powerful of all forms of enthusiasm.

- Enthusiasm is the twin brother of the faculty of the will, it being the major source of sustained action of the will. It is also a sustaining force in connection with persistence. We might say, therefore, that willpower, persistence and enthusiasm are triplets which give one sustained action with a minimum of loss of physical energy. Emerson spoke no greater truth than this: "Nothing great was ever achieved without enthusiasm."

Mr. Carnegie then proceeded to demonstrate how enthusiasm may be applied, as follows:

> Take the professional author as an example: A man's writing may be translated into many languages, but it will always carry with it the same tempo of enthusiasm the writer felt when he was writing, and that enthusiasm will be detected by the reader.
>
> I have heard it said that the writer of advertisements, who feels no enthusiasm in connection with his copy, writes poor copy, no matter how many facts he may reveal.
>
> I have also heard that the lawyer who feels no enthusiasm over his case fails to convince judges and juries. And there is plenty of evidence that the enthusiasm of a doctor is his greatest remedy in the sick room.
>
> Also, enthusiasm is one of the greatest builders of confidence, for everyone knows that enthusiasm

and faith are related. Enthusiasm connotes hope and courage and belief in one's self. I do not recall having ever promoted a man to a higher position, or having ever employed a man for a responsible position of any sort, who had not first demonstrated his enthusiasm over the possibilities of the position.

Enthusiasm connotes hope and courage and belief in one's self.

I have observed that young men and young women who have gone to work in our offices, as clerks and stenographers, have promoted themselves into more responsible positions in almost exact ratio to the enthusiasm they expressed in their work. You cannot hold an enthusiastic man down very long, even if you desired to do so, for enthusiasm is like water in a dam; you can control it for a time but it will always break out somewhere.

But, I must warn you that self-discipline is necessary, because uncontrolled enthusiasm often is as detrimental as no enthusiasm at all. For example, the man who is so enthusiastic over himself and his own ideas that he monopolizes the conversation when he converses with others is sure to be unpopular, not to mention the fact that he misses many opportunities to learn by listening to others.

Then, there is the man who becomes too enthusiastic over the roulette wheel or the horses; and the man who becomes more enthusiastic over ways and means of getting something for nothing than he does over rendering useful service; and the woman who becomes more enthusiastic over card parties and "society" than she does over making her home and herself attractive to her husband. This sort of uncontrolled enthusiasm may be very detrimental to all whom it affects.

Mr. Carnegie, asked if enthusiasm could be of any value to a man engaged in ordinary manual labor, replied:

I can best answer that question by calling your attention to the fact that most of the higher officials of my own organization began in the humblest sort of jobs. The man who made the greatest progress of all my associates began as a day laborer, and he worked as a teamster before he came with us. His boundless enthusiasm was the quality which enabled him to lift himself, step by step, into the highest position I had to offer. His name was Charles M. Schwab, and the position to which he lifted himself, by his enthusiasm, was that of president of the United States Steel Corporation, at a salary of $75,000 a year. (In 1901, 39-year-old Schwab, during his two-year stint at the head of U.S. Steel, Schwab earned more than $2 million annually.[1])

Yes, enthusiasm can be of value to anyone, regardless of his occupation, for it is a quality which attracts favorable attention, makes friends, establishes confidence, and breaks down the opposition of others.

Mr. Carnegie also gave me his opinion of the part enthusiasm plays in the home relationship of men and women:

Let us first go back a little beyond the home relationship, and consider the part which enthusiasm plays in bringing men and women together in the bond of marriage. Did you ever hear of a man winning the woman of his choice without displaying great enthusiasm over her? I believe they call it "love"! And it also works the other way around. A man will not be inclined to propose marriage to the woman who shows no enthusiasm over him. Mutual enthusiasm, therefore, is the basis of marriage, and woe will be the lot of that party to any marriage who allows enthusiasm to wane after marriage. We speak of the emotion of love, but what is love but mutual enthusiasm of two people expressed toward one another?

Enthusiasm is perhaps the most misunderstood word in the English language, for there are but a few who recognize that the so called genius is only a man who, because of his great capacity for enthusiasm, steps up the power of his mind until he is enabled to communicate with a source of knowledge which is not available to him through his faculty of reason alone.

Some so-called enthusiasm is nothing but an uncontrolled expression of one's ego–a state of mental excitement which is easily recognized as only a meaningless expression of personal vanity. This kind of enthusiasm may be very detrimental to those who indulge in it, as they usually express themselves through some form of exaggeration.

Mr. Carnegie was then requested by me to give further details as to how men may promote themselves into better positions through the expression of enthusiasm. He explained:

To begin with, let us take note of the fact that a man's mental attitude, whether it is negative or positive, spreads to the minds of his associates, and becomes, also, their mental attitude. I have known one man, with a negative state of mind, to influence the minds of a thousand others who were working in the same plant, without his having spoken a word to the others. You can readily see, therefore, why a man with a negative mind is not an asset to any organization, no matter how skilled he may be in his work.

Any state of mind is contagious!

And there is a law of nature which makes a man's thought habits permanent. That same law also conveys one's thoughts to the minds of others. This explains why an employee with a positive mind is worth more than one with a negative mind. The employee who thinks, speaks and acts in terms of enthusiasm is one who is happy in his work. He therefore radiates a wholesome influence which spreads to those around him, and they take on a part of his mental attitude.

*Enthusiasm gives you
a keener imagination,
increases personal
initiative, makes you
more alert, and gives you
a pleasing personality,
all of which attract the
friendly cooperation
of other people.*

But this is not the only reason why the person who expresses enthusiasm promotes himself into the more desirable positions of life. Enthusiasm gives one a keener imagination, increases his personal initiative, makes him more alert in mind, gives him a pleasing personality, and these qualities attract the friendly cooperation of other people. These traits of

mind make it inevitable that the individual will promote himself into any position which he is capable
of filling,

Also, every thought one releases becomes a definite part of his character. This takes place through
the principle of auto-suggestion. One does not have
to be a mathematician to figure out what will happen
to the person whose dominating thoughts are always
positive, for obviously such a person adds power to
his own character with every thought he releases.

Thought by thought he builds up a personality which provides him with a strong will, a keen
imagination, self-reliance, persistence, personal initiative and the courage and ambition to desire, and
to acquire, whatever he chooses. An employer has
but little to do with the promotion of such a person.
If one employer neglects to recognize his ability,
he finds another one who will, but he manages to
keep on growing and advancing in any direction he
chooses.

The influence which one person projects to the
minds of those nearest him is obvious in every place
of business. Take the retail store, for example, and
you will observe that the mental attitude of the
owner or the manager is definitely reflected in every
employee of the store. It has been said that a skilled
psychologist can walk through any retail store,
study the employees a few minutes, and then give a

surprisingly accurate description of the dominating head of the store, without seeing him or knowing anything about him except that which he feels and observes in the store.

The same thing is possible in the home, or any other place where people gather and become associated regularly. The trained psychologist can go into any home, get the "mental feel" of the place, and tell precisely whether the home is dominated by the spirit of harmony or the spirit of bickering and friction. The mental attitude of the people who live there leaves its permanent influence in the very atmosphere of the place.

Every city has its own rate of personality, made up of the dominating influences and the mental attitude of the people who live there. Moreover, every street, and every block in every street, also has its own personality, each being so different that the trained psychologist can walk down any street, blindfolded, and pick up enough information to enable him to give an accurate description of the people who live there.

There is, as I have stated, a natural law which fixes the habits of thought and tends to give them permanency. This law not only gives permanency to the habits of thought in the mind of the individual, but it projects the influences of that thought to the environment in which the individual lives.

Not only the trained psychologist, but practically everyone, tunes in on the vibrations of thought which other people release, and most people judge others very largely by the "mental feel" they pick up when in the presence of others, although they often do this unconsciously.

Whether we are conscious of this fact or not, we all have the habit of judging others by their personal appearance and the "mental feel" we pick up when we contact them. Personal appearances can be misleading, but the "mental feel" never is. Both media are important.

People's personal appearance is an accurate insight into what is in their minds.

The military officials of the United States Army are very particular about the personal appearance of the soldiers under their command. They know, from experience, that men who are slovenly and careless about their personal appearance are apt to be careless, also, about their mental habits. That is why both the army and the navy have regular inspection periods when everyone is carefully looked over. Personal appearances give an accurate insight into what takes place in the minds of the soldiers and sailors.

The same rule applies, less strictly perhaps, in the field of business. Some retail stores, for instance, are so particular about the personal appearance of their salespeople that they, too, have regular inspection periods. They have learned from experience that the public judges a store very largely by the appearance of its salespeople.

Many employees have attracted attention to themselves, and have gained promotions, because of their neat personal appearance. Of course, the promotion was not based upon the appearance alone, but appearance was an important factor which connoted other qualities that go along with personal appearance.

The person who is lacking in enthusiasm publicizes his weakness in many different ways–by the tone of his voice, the posture of his body, the way he carries himself when walking, and his personal adornment. The alert, enthusiastic person carefully watches all of these signs of character, and it is hardly necessary to suggest that he gets along better than the person who does not.

And I might add that this rule applies to domestic animals and to the birds and beasts of wild-life, the same as to man. The finer specimens take great care with their physical appearance. The song birds keep their feathers clean and neatly arranged, while the more slovenly birds, such as the buzzard, pay less attention to their physical appearance.

That old saying that "cleanliness is next to God-liness" is by no means a mere figure of speech. The more spirited creatures of the earth reflect the nature of their spirit by their physical appearance and their environmental habits.

QUESTIONS TO CONSIDER...

1. Of the several people quoted in the beginning of this chapter, which quote resonated with you the most deeply? The least?

2. "Our mental attitude, our heart's desire, is our perpetual prayer that Nature answers." Rewrite this quote in your own words, in detail. Then cite your personal "burning desire," providing your reason why this desire is so important to you.

3. Because enthusiasm is the major factor to convert negative emotion into positive emotion and prepares the mind for the development and expression of Faith, will you determine to become more enthusiastic in the future? Specifically why? Or why not?

4. When are you the most enthusiastic? For examples: When you are at home with family? When you are speaking to a client/customer? When you are watching a sports activity? When you are preparing a presentation? How does your enthusiasm affect your attitude?

5. Which of Andrew Carnegie's wisdom quotations stood out to you the most? What about that quote made you stop and think twice about it?

2

FACTORS THAT DESTROY ENTHUSIASM

M r. Carnegie was requested to mention some of the influences that discourage enthusiasm. This is his description:

First on the list perhaps is poverty. It has been said that when poverty comes in the front door, hope, ambition, courage, personal initiative and enthusiasm take to their heels and run out the back door. I believe this is not an exaggeration of fact.

Physical illness holds a top position as a destroyer of enthusiasm. It is difficult for anyone to express enthusiasm over anything when he is physically or mentally ill.

Failure in business also holds a high ranking position as a destroyer of enthusiasm. Those who have not learned the art of converting failure into renewed effort usually allow the failure to drown out their spirit of enthusiasm, which is the equivalent of saying that they thereby condemn themselves to permanent failure.

Disappointment in affairs of the heart is not exactly food for enthusiasm. I have never yet seen the person who could display convincing signs of genuine enthusiasm while suffering from this kind of disappointment. It is one of the more common causes of permanent failure.

Family disputes, especially those which too often take place between the heads of the family, are also death to enthusiasm. It is difficult for a man to display enthusiasm in connection with his job, or his business, or his profession, if he knows that a family argument awaits his homecoming at the end of the day, or if he leaves the breakfast table in the morning following a row with his wife, or with some other member of his family.

Lack of education sometimes serves as a killer of enthusiasm, as it often leads to the development of an inferiority complex, and this despite the fact that some of the most successful men the world has ever known were men with but little education. Lack of opportunity for self-advancement rates along with poverty as a dampener of enthusiasm.

And unfriendly criticism causes most people to go into their shells of silence, and to place their enthusiasm in cold storage the moment they are criticized, or they become cynical, rebellious and strike back at their critics.

And unfriendly criticism causes most people to retreat into shells of silence, and place their enthusiasm in cold storage.

Old age is looked upon by some people not as an approach to greater wisdom, but as a sign of decline in ability, and away goes their enthusiasm, its place being taken by fear and worry. Worry and doubt and fear are three killers of enthusiasm which have no equal in destructiveness. Where these unholy triplets appear, ambition takes to its wings in a hurry, and poverty and misery move in. To be a habitual enthusiast, one must be a strong believer in something constructive. Unbelievers are negative, and unbelief becomes a habit. Worry is the child of doubt. It grows out of indecision and inaction.

A negative mental attitude, no matter what may be its cause, makes enthusiasm impossible. Enthusiasm simply will not fraternize with a negative mind. The habit of association with negative minded people is also a killer of enthusiasm. No one can long maintain a spirit of enthusiasm while associating with pessimists and cynics and those who live without hope.

Enthusiasm is an expression of hope, faith, belief and the will to win, expressed through Definiteness of Purpose. Enthusiasm can be developed through action appropriate to its nature, but it cannot be developed by mere wishing or daydreaming. There must be action behind it!

When a man gets an obsessional desire to attain a definite purpose, and pitches in with everything he has to attain that purpose, the action feature of his desire evolves into enthusiasm. All forms

Enthusiasm is an expression of hope, faith, belief, and the will to win, expressed through Definiteness of Purpose.

of enthusiasm are the result of motive expressed through action.

Here you have a catalogue of the major causes of lack of enthusiasm, presented by a man who converted his own enthusiasm into the United States of America's greatest industrial enterprise. Study the list carefully.

ENTHUSIASM AND THE MASTER MIND

I asked Mr. Carnegie to state what part enthusiasm plays in the maintenance of a Master Mind group. He replied:

> A Master Mind group should consist of men with creative vision who can create practical ideas and plan objectives; but it should include, also, sound critics of ideas, the two types of minds working together in a spirit of harmony.
>
> Every Master Mind group should have at least one "wet blanket" man to question and test the ideas of the other members of the group. The "wet blanket" man should anticipate all the weaknesses of the objectives and of the plans by which they are to be attained. He should see the hole in the doughnut, but allow the other members of the group to see the doughnut around the hole. He may not be as popular

as the other members of the group, but he will be just as useful.

Enthusiasm is the first requirement of a master salesman, but experience has proved that the ablest sales managers are not the greatest enthusiasts. They organize, plan and direct, but never allow their enthusiasm to outweigh their reasoning power. Many fine sales organizations have been ruined by placing at their head men whose enthusiasm was greater than their judgment.

One of the major weaknesses of most individuals who are inspired by great enthusiasm consists in their lack of a dependable means of controlling their enthusiasm, through the influence of a constructive critic. The criticism should be constructive analysis rather than negative criticism or fault finding.

Every well-managed purchasing department has at its head a man who has his enthusiasm under control at all times. His business is to resist the enthusiasm of the salesmen with whom he must deal, not to embrace it and be swept away by it. Cool judgment and experience are his constant companions, his greatest assets.

When a man gets into a "buying mood," as many individuals do, he is apt to buy more than he can conveniently pay for. This "buying mood" is one of the major weaknesses of many people, especially those who buy on the monthly payment plan. Whenever I feel myself getting into this mood, I hasten to find my "wet blanket" man, so he may cool me off a bit before I go too far. Enthusiasm belongs on the selling side of the counter, not on the buying side!

And this rule applies as definitely when a man is buying another man's ideas as when he is buying the other man's merchandise! Most of us can give testimony in support of this truth, for rarely can a man be found who has not, at one time or another, "bought" some other fellow's ideas to his own detriment and regret.

Enthusiasm is a priceless asset, but it is an asset only when it is under control at all times. In a well-managed business it is understood that both the enthusiast and his balance wheel, the "wet blanket" man, are essential. You understand, of course, that professional analysis is a far different thing from voluntary, uninvited criticism. Professional analysis is, or should be, accepted in a spirit of friendly cooperation, for the benefit of all whom it affects.

Personal criticism, of the usual type, is nothing less than an expression of antagonism or disapproval. Such criticism is highly destructive. I do not recall having ever criticized another man in this spirit. When I find it necessary to analyze a man's mistakes—I'm speaking of my own associates of course—I always prepare the way very carefully and approach the subject cautiously, by asking questions which force answers that lead to self-admission of mistakes.

I have found this plan to work better than direct criticism. It never leaves a man with a bad taste in his mouth, nor a negative mental attitude in his mind. It is surprising how frankly men will admit their own mistakes if they are maneuvered into a position where they can become their own critics. The Chinese call this "face-saving." It gives a man an opportunity to admit his mistakes without the loss of his pride, and one self-admitted mistake is about the same as a corrected mistake.

Let me give you an example of an experience I had in face-saving: My personal secretary was a young man who had been with me for several years. He was efficient, had a pleasing personality, and he was dependable; but he fell in with a group of young people who had the bad habit of getting their enthusiasm out of a whiskey bottle, and the first thing I knew he began to show up at the office late on Monday mornings.

Then he began to show signs of irritability, and I knew the time had come for me to do a little friendly analysis on his behalf, so I prepared the way by inviting him out to my house for dinner.

We prepared an especially nice "company" dinner, and during the meal hour we chatted pleasantly about everything except the subject I had in mind discussing with him.

After dinner we went into the library and lit our cigars. The stage was then ready for the show, so I began by asking him a few questions. First, I asked him if he believed that a man who drank liquor regularly should be considered for promotion to a higher position. He said he thought not.

Then I asked him what he would do if he had in his employ a man who had become so addicted to the liquor habit that he could not get to work on time. He replied that he probably would fire him.

By this time the young man had begun to squirm in his chair, showing clearly that he recognized he was being slowly pushed out on a limb. I waited a few moments, while he "stewed in his own fat," and then I asked him if he thought it might not be possible that a sensible man could change his habits in time to save himself from ruin.

Now he was on the very tip of the limb, holding on for dear life. He waited for a couple of minutes before answering; then straightened himself, looked me squarely in the eyes, and said, "You needn't go any further! I have known for a long time that this hour was coming, and I deeply appreciate your kindness in making it as easy for me as possible. All I can say is that I have been a fool, but I can change, and I will do so if you will bear with me long enough to let me prove it."

Of course, I gave him the chance. That was the last I heard of his drinking habits. He had been disciplined, but it was self-discipline. I never said a word to him which might have been construed as criticism.

That young man took a new hold on his job, with renewed spirit, and promoted himself from one position to another until he became the manager of one of our largest steel plants. Later he left our service and went into business for himself, and I supplied a portion of the capital for that business. His business venture turned out to be very profitable; therefore, the constructive analysis paid both of us, whereas destructive criticism could have harmed us both.

Here we have a description of the technique through which a great builder of business executives administered discipline through "criticism" without destroying enthusiasm.

Every foreman and supervisor might well afford to learn Mr. Carnegie's description by heart, as it is a smart person indeed who can maneuver others into admitting their own weaknesses and curing them by their own initiative.

THE RELATIONSHIP OF ENTHUSIASM AND PRAYER

We come now to one of the effects of enthusiasm that is of the utmost importance to every person who believes in the efficacy of prayer.

It has been observed, by psychologists and laymen alike, that intense, controlled enthusiasm increases the power of thought so that the motivated mind projects itself into the deeper recesses of Infinite Intelligence.

Unusual phenomena have been known to result when the enthusiasm has been intensified to the proportions of self-hypnosis; and distinguished inventors including Thomas A. Edison and Dr. Elmer R. Gates, have freely admitted that many of their more complex problems were solved by this method of mind control.

The technique through which enthusiasm may be intensified is as follows:

- The mind is fixed upon a definite purpose.

- Through applied faith, that purpose is fanned into a white heat of burning desire for its attainment.

- Through self-discipline and controlled attention, the mind is focused upon the purpose and held there with persistence.

- By the application of these four principles—Definiteness of Purpose, Applied Faith, Self-Discipline, and

Controlled Attention–the spirit of enthusiasm is developed to the proportions of self-hypnosis.

Do not become alarmed over that word "hypnosis," for it is a well-known fact that all great leaders, whatever their calling may be, spur themselves onward, either consciously or unconsciously, by self-hypnosis. The capacity to do so is the major difference between a great leader and a mediocre leader.

The subject of hypnosis has gained a bad reputation because of the charlatans who have abused it. That does not alter the principle of hypnosis any more than the abuse of the emotion of love alters that principle. Both are the gifts of the Creator to mankind, and both have their legitimate purpose or they would not exist.

Enthusiasm is the action-producing feature of faith.

The emotional feeling of enthusiasm has the effect of clearing the mind of negative thoughts, thus preparing the way for the expression of that state of mind known as Faith. Enthusiasm is the "action-producing" feature of Faith. Without this action, Faith is passive and serves no purpose. "Faith without works is dead," as one philosopher has stated the truth.

It has been recognized that prayers that are not accompanied by a burning desire produce only negative results of disappointment. A burning desire is nothing but intensified enthusiasm! And we may as well recognize the truth that all prayers that produce positive results are administered through the spirit of enthusiasm and self-hypnosis, for it is an indisputable truth.

Now we are beginning to get a broader understanding of the powers of enthusiasm that ignites motivation! We are beginning to recognize the truth that it is something more than an emotional feeling which, all too often, is expressed in terms of small talk and foolish laughter.

Yes, we are beginning to recognize the truth that enthusiasm is a close relative of faith; that it is a state of mind clearing the way for faith, and gives to faith its action qualities. This is something far different from the average person's idea of enthusiasm, isn't it?

Now let us examine still another important truth: When you adopt a Definite Major Purpose and concentrate your mind upon its attainment, with a burning desire, you very soon reach the point where you expect the object of your desire to be attained.

By continued concentration upon the desire, that belief becomes translated into faith. This takes place through some strange power inherent in every mind, a power that has never been isolated or analyzed, but is a recognizable power nevertheless.

The important feature to remember is the fact that an ordinary desire, or a Definite Major Purpose, may be translated into faith by the simple process of stepping up the power of thought, through enthusiasm, until that desire becomes a burning desire!

When enthusiasm becomes so great that it enables you to have enough faith to see (through your imagination) yourself already in possession of the objects of your desire, before you have actually obtained physical possession, you experience precisely the same results if you called your desires a prayer! The procedure brings results under one name as quickly as it does under any other.

Fear, doubt, indefiniteness of purpose, and lack of enthusiasm always produce negative results.

Fear, doubt, indefiniteness of purpose, and lack of enthusiasm always produce negative results. If the mind is dominated by any one of these negatives, or any other negative thought, the results will be negative.

It is impressively significant that lack of enthusiasm ends in negative results in connection with both the principle of definiteness of purpose, and the more profound expression of desires through what is known as prayer.

ENTHUSIASM IN THE HOME

The spiritual foundation of the nation centers in the American home, where the character of individuals is shaped and developed. Therefore, let us turn our attention to inspired feeling as it may affect the home, for we shall find that here, also, controlled enthusiasm is an important factor that may determine, to a large degree, the destiny of every member of the family,

A little more than forty-five years ago, a farmer living in the mountain section of one of the Southern states brought home a new wife, to become the stepmother of his two small boys. The wife brought with her two sons of her own. In due time, a fifth son was born of the marriage.

The home was one of the more humble types, which are so typical of the mountain country. The farmer was the product of four generations of his people, who had been born and reared in that community, in surroundings of poverty and illiteracy.

His wife came from a more prosperous section of the state, and she had received the benefits of a cultural background and a college education. Therefore, she was not the type to accept poverty and illiteracy without protest.

The evening that the farmer brought his new wife home he introduced her to all the older relatives who had gathered at his home for the wedding reception, ending with an introduction to his eldest son, a lad of nine years of age, whom he introduced in these words: "And now I wish you to meet this fellow who is distinguished for being the worst boy in this county, and he will probably start throwing rocks at you not later than tomorrow morning."

The stepmother went over to the young "Jesse James," placed her hand under his chin, tilted his head upward, looked him squarely in the eyes for a moment, then turned to her husband and said: "No! You are wrong. This is not the worst boy in the county; he is the smartest boy in the county who has not yet found the proper outlet for his enthusiasm."

Then and there began a friendship between that young lad and his stepmother, which was destined to project its influence for good throughout more than half of the civilized world. That was the first time anyone had ever called the boy "smart." His relatives, including his father and all the neighbors, had built him up in his own mind as being a bad boy and he had tried not to disappoint them.

But this stepmother, in one brief sentence, changed all that!

Think of this story, you fathers and mothers, and you who have it within your power to influence youngsters. It may inspire you to work miracles in the lives of some who need only the right influence to give them a start on the road that leads to happiness.

The stepmother was a small woman, weighing only 105 pounds, but what she lacked in avoirdupois (weight) she more than made up in ambition and enthusiasm. Shortly after she came into that poverty stricken mountain home she held a "Master Mind" meeting with her husband, which was destined to force him to forever part company with poverty. At the end of the meeting it was announced that he was to be sent away to a dental college. The following year he matriculated, at the age of thirty eight, at the Louisville Dental College, of Louisville, Kentucky, where he remained until he graduated.

The dental education had been decided upon because the wife had done a bit of encouragement after she came into that mountain home, from which she learned that her husband was quite a fair mechanic, having done considerable work in his father's blacksmith shop, shoeing horses, sharpening plows and the like. She decided that this mechanical ability could just as well be directed to the field of dentistry.

The farmer protested at first, but to no avail. The wife's enthusiasm was greater than his alibis, so dentistry it became! Her judgment was confirmed by the fact that the farmer led all his classes in dental school, completed the course in three years, which takes most students four years, and carried away with him the highest honors awarded to any student by the college.

Upon his return home from dental college his wife turned on her enthusiasm once more, and influenced him to move his home and his dental office to the county seat, where he would have a better clientele for the practice of his profession.

Again, he protested, and again, his wife's enthusiasm came out victorious.

They moved to the county seat, and the erstwhile poverty stricken farmer became one of the most successful and prosperous men of the county.

By this time the fifth son had been born and the four sons by the previous marriages of the farmer and his wife had grown up to be fair sized lads; the eldest of them–the young "Jesse James"– having reached his fourteenth year.

It was time now for the stepmother to prove the soundness of the opinion she expressed of this boy the first time she saw him. So she called him into the parlor, closed the doors, and went into a Master Mind meeting with him.

Before that meeting was over she had transplanted some of her enthusiasm into his mind, in the form of a Definite Major Purpose, consisting of a decision to become an author.

He began, under his stepmother's guidance, to write local news items for small town papers. In a little while, he had built up a clientele of more than a dozen papers, some of which paid him with a "free" subscription to their papers, others with small stipends that usually came in the form of postage stamps.

But, a start had been made in the right direction, and that was important. The young "Jesse James" had been influenced to lay aside his pistol (an item of personal possession with which he was well supplied when his stepmother came upon the scene) and to discover the superior power of the pen–a power he wielded wisely and effectively.

Thus, the small seedling of enthusiasm planted in his mind by his stepmother, when he was a small boy, has been extended until it is now serving men and women in almost every walk of life, through the teaching of the philosophy of success you are now hearing about.

A part of that same enthusiasm was planted in the minds of his four brothers, who are likewise rendering useful service on a large scale. One is a physician, one is a dentist, one is the president of a college, and the fourth is a lawyer.

Yes, enthusiasm has power! When that power is released behind Definiteness of Purpose, and backed by faith, it multiplies itself until it becomes an irresistible power, for which poverty and temporary defeat are no match.

And it is a power that may be touched off in the mind of any person with very little effort. In reality, the part played by the stepmother of the mountain bred "bad" boy was not great within itself. It consisted mainly in the planting of the seed of Definiteness of Purpose and of fertilizing that seed with the spirit of her enthusiasm.

Perhaps that is the greatest service anyone can render another, for enthusiasm is a contagious force, and once it has been transplanted into a new field it spreads and grows of its own accord, provided it is accompanied by Definiteness of Purpose.

Enthusiasm is related to every faculty of the mind. It is in fact the action-producing factor of the mind. It touches off the faculty

Enthusiasm is a contagious force that multiplies when accompanied by Definiteness of Purpose and backed by faith.

of the imagination and inspires creative vision and the exercise of personal initiative. And it arouses the subconscious section of the mind to greater activity, inspiring it to project itself deeply into the reservoirs of Infinite Intelligence, where the answers to all human problems exist.

Thus, enthusiasm is literally the gateway of approach to your spiritual qualities. It not only gives deep conviction to the words you speak, but it projects its influence into the inner recesses of your soul.

It is not surprising, therefore, that Ralph Waldo Emerson said, "Nothing great was ever achieved without enthusiasm," for he had felt the influence of his enthusiasm in his own soul, where it revealed to him the hidden forces of his being and made his name immortal among the philosophers of the world.

And it was this same influence of her own enthusiasm which reached deeply into the soul of Helen Keller and inspired her with the faith through which she mastered her afflictions of being unable to hear, speak, or see.

Enthusiasm carried the great Thomas Edison through ten thousand failures and revealed to him, at long last, the secret of the incandescent electric lamp. Psychologists who have studied Edison's achievements all agree that his astounding physical endurance, which was so great that he often got along on four hours of sleep per day, was inspired by his enduring enthusiasm over his Definite Major Purpose.

This same power inspired George Washington with the faith to keep on fighting, in the face of what seemed to be insurmountable obstacles, until he won the freedom and liberty the people of the United States now enjoy.

And enthusiasm was the power that inspired the people of the United States to awaken and prepare themselves to meet their greatest emergency, at the outbreak of World War II, an achievement that astounded the entire world because of the efficiency and dispatch.

Enthusiasm was the power that sustained Abraham Lincoln during the War Between the States, and enabled him to carry on until he saved this nation from self-destruction.

How can this power be attained?

The procedure is simple; it is within the control of everyone, as the Creator intended it should be.

You start with hope—the hope of achievement of some definite end. Hope is the forerunner of faith. Where there is no hope there can be no faith. That is obvious.

The smoldering embers of hope may be fanned into the white flame of faith by feeding them with controlled enthusiasm, backed by definiteness of purpose. The fanning process should be kept up until ordinary desire becomes a burning desire.

When hope, enthusiasm, and faith are combined through definiteness of purpose, they give you access to unlimited mind power.

First comes hope, the result of desire based on a definite purpose; then follows the active expression of hope, through enthusiasm. These ripen into faith, the state of mind that masters all forms of defeat and overcomes all opposition.

Hope, enthusiasm, and faith are key because of their close relationship. When they are combined through definiteness of purpose, they give you access to unlimited mind power.

NOTE

1. Charles M. Schwab, *Britannica;* https://www.britannica.com/ biography/Charles-M-Schwab; accessed November 29, 2023.

QUESTIONS TO CONSIDER...

1. By applying these four principles–Definiteness of Purpose, Applied Faith, Self-Discipline, and Controlled Attention–the spirit of enthusiasm is developed to the proportions of self-hypnosis. What does this statement mean to you on a personal level? How do you define "self-hypnosis"?

2. Of the seven fears that destroy enthusiasm–poverty, criticism, ill health, love loss, old age, loss of freedom, death–which one or two are your greatest fear(s)? What steps have you taken to overcome this fear?

3. Why should every Master Mind group have at least one "wet blanket"?

4. Enthusiasm is the action-producing factor of your mind–it provokes imagination, inspires creative vision and personal initiative, arouses the subconscious to greater activity, and affects the deep reservoirs of Infinite Intelligence, where the answers to all human problems exist. Do you agree? Disagree? Explain.

5. How closely related is your hope, enthusiasm, and faith? Are you purposely focused on combining these three keys through definiteness of purpose to access unlimited mind power to achieve your goals?

3

CULTIVATING A POSITIVE MENTAL ATTITUDE

Whatever your mind can conceive and believe,
your mind can and will achieve.
–Napoleon Hill

At the time of birth, each human being brings with him the equivalent of two sealed envelopes in which appear a list of the *riches* he may enjoy by taking possession of his own mind and using it for the attainment of what he desires in life–and a list of the *penalties* that Nature will exact from him if he neglects to recognize and use his own mind power.

In this chapter, I break the seal of these two envelopes and present you with the contents; but more important than this, I suggest that you discover for yourself that these sealed envelopes are not imaginary, but real—and that they may be the means of putting you on the success beam where you can ride to victory and a destination of your own choosing.

There are two things Nature definitely discourages and severely penalizes: (1) A vacuum (emptiness) and (2) idleness (lack of action). Remove from active use any muscle of the body and it will atrophy and become useless. Tie an arm to your side and remove it from action and it, in time, will wither and become useless.

The same law that governs other portions of the physical body governs the brain, where the powers of thought are organized and released. You either use your brain for controlled thinking in connection with things you want, or nature steps in and uses it to grow you a marvelous crop of negative circumstances you do not want.

You have a choice in this connection: you can take possession of your thought power or you can let it be influenced by all the stray winds of chance and circumstances you do not desire.

You can make your mind dwell on positive thinking, or you can let it drift to negative thinking, but you cannot sit idly by and thereby free yourself from the influence of those two sealed envelopes. You either embrace the one marked *Riches* and follow its instructions, or you are forced to suffer the *Penalties* of the other.

Out of this great truth has grown the saying "success attracts more success while failure attracts more failure," a truth you probably have observed many times, although you may not have analyzed the cause back of it.

The cause is very simple: Nature allows you to fix your mind on whatever you desire and create your own plan for attaining it, then places back of your efforts all those benefits that come to you in that sealed envelope labeled *Riches,* which you may have in return for taking possession of your own mind and directing it to ends of your own choosing.

Thus, it is clear as to why success attracts more success once you have placed yourself on the success beam. It is also equally clear why failure attracts more failure if, by neglect, you have not taken possession of your mind and put it to work. Truly, Nature discourages idleness and penalizes it wherever it exists.

With a Positive Mental Attitude, you can put your mind to work believing in success and your belief will guide you to success.

With a Positive Mental Attitude, you can put your mind to work believing in success and opulence as your right, and your belief will guide you unerringly toward whatever your definition of these may be.

With that same mind operating through a negative mental attitude, you can believe in fear and frustration and your mind will attract to you the fruits of these undesirable states of mind.

Or, you can make no attempt to control and direct your mind and it will be wide open to every influence you come into contact with–yielding you only the things you do not want, the things mentioned in that sealed envelope labeled *penalties*. You must pay for neglecting to take possession of your mind and direct it.

Now let us break down the contents of these two sealed envelopes and see what they contain. We will call one of these envelopes *rewards* and the other *penalties*. In the one labeled *rewards* is a list of some of the blessings it brings those who embrace and use the principle of a Positive Mental Attitude. These rewards include:

1. The privilege of placing yourself on the success beam that attracts only the circumstances that lead to success.

2. Sound health, both physically and mentally.

3. Financial independence.

4. A labor of love in which to express yourself.

5. Peace of mind.

6. Applied Faith that makes fear impossible.

7. Enduring friendships.

8. Longevity and a well-balanced life.

9. Immunity against all forms of self-limitation.

10. The wisdom to understand yourself and others.

These are some of the blessings, but not all of them, listed in that sealed envelope.

Now let us examine the envelope labeled *penalties:*

1. Poverty and misery all your life.

2. Mental and physical ailments of many kinds.

3. Self-limitations that bind you to mediocrity all the days of your life.

4. Fear in all its destructive forms.

5. Dislike for your occupation, your means of earning a living.

6. Many enemies, few friends.

7. Every brand of worry known to mankind.

8. A victim of every negative influence you encounter.

9. Subject to the influence and control of other people at their will.

10. A wasted life that gives nothing to the betterment of mankind.

There is your catalogue of rewards and penalties!

You must embrace and use the one or have the other forced upon you! There is no halfway point, no means of compromise, so you are on trial as a citizen of life, and you are the judge and the jury, the attorney for the defense and the prosecutor. The final verdict, therefore, as to what happens to you throughout life will be of your own making and there is no higher Court of Appeals in this world.

HOW IMPORTANT IS A POSITIVE MENTAL ATTITUDE?

Let's take inventory and determine just how important a Positive Mental Attitude (PMA) can be.

PMA is the first and the most important step we must take to create, control, and direct a motivated mind. A negative mental attitude leaves us wide open to harmful influences.

PMA is the only condition of the mind that we can:

• Benefit from the rewards coming with us in the sealed envelope.

- Access the success beam and remain there.

- Develop and maintain a good health consciousness.

- Give ourselves complete protection against all fears and sources of worry.

- Express Applied Faith and draw upon the forces of Infinite Intelligence at will; therefore it is the foundation of all our prayers.

- Meet and recognize our "other self," which has no self-limitation and remains always in our possession to direct it to desired ends and finds an answer for each of our problems.

- Express the great creative emotion of love, the master healer of our physical and spiritual wounds and the medicine that aids our souls in times of trial and distress.

- Write our own tickets in life and be sure of making life pay off in dividends of our own choosing.

- Gain the wisdom to recognize the true purpose of life and adapt ourselves to that purpose.

Will you join with me, therefore, in saying that a Positive Mental Attitude is a "must" for all who make life pay off on their own terms?

STEPS TO TAKE TO DEVELOP A POSITIVE MENTAL ATTITUDE AND CREATE A MOTIVATED MINDSET

1. Recognize your privilege of taking possession of and using your mind as being the only thing over which you have complete control; this being a necessary step before you can benefit from the wisdom in this book.

2. Recognize the truth that every adversity, failure, defeat, sorrow, and unpleasant circumstance carries with it the seed of an equivalent benefit that may be transmuted into a blessing of great proportions.

3. Learn to close the door behind you on the failures and unpleasant circumstances you may have experienced in the past, thus clearing the way in your mind for a Positive Mental Attitude.

4. Select the most important person in the world, past or present, from your point of view, and make that person your pace-maker for the remainder of your life, emulating him or her in every possible way.

5. Determine how many material riches you require, set up a plan for acquiring them, then place a stop gap on your ambitions to be richer by adopting the principle of not too much, not too little by which to guide your future ambitions for material things.

(Greed for overabundance of material things has destroyed more people than any other one cause.)

6. Form the habit of daily saying or doing something to make another person(s) feel better, if it is nothing more than making a phone call or writing a post card (email, text). An autographed copy of a good inspirational book placed in the hands of one who needs it could work wonders for you, even if the person to whom you give it never reads it.

That which you do to or for another, you do to or for yourself.

Please keep in mind the fact that I am here giving you instructions on how to condition your mind so it will maintain and express a Positive Mental Attitude automatically, at all times. In addition to the six listed, the following are actions to seriously consider, take to heart, and then take action:

Find out what you like best to do—discover a labor of love—and do it with all your heart and soul, even if it is only a hobby. Idle hands and idle minds are said to be the devil's favorite tools, which he uses to keep people thinking negatively.

Learn that when you meet with a personal problem that you haven't been able to solve, look around and find someone with a similar or greater problem and help that person to find the solution. By the time the solution is found, the solution to your own problem will also be found.

Read Emerson's *Essay on Compensation* once a week until you understand and assimilate it, and discover that it ranks high in the scale of influences with which you can condition your mind for a Positive Mental Attitude.

Take a complete inventory of every asset you possess, exclusive of material riches, and discover that your greatest asset is a sound mind with which you can shape your own destiny by the simple process of taking full possession of it and directing it to ends of your own choice.

Communicate with anyone you have unjustly offended, by word or deed, and offer adequate apologies and ask forgiveness. The more bitter this assignment may seem, the greater will be your rewards for carrying it out.

Recognize that the space you occupy in this world is in exact ratio to the quality and the quantity of the service you render for the benefit of others, plus your mental attitude.

Remember, always, that no one can hurt your feelings or make you angry or frighten you without your full cooperation and consent. You can close your mind to all who endeavor to enter it for destructive purposes—you are "the master of your fate, the captain of your soul." (Quote from *Invictus* by William Ernest Henley.)

Discover that self-pity is an insidious destroyer of self-reliance and that the one person on whom you can and should depend at all times is yourself. Whether you write, preach sermons, sell merchandise or services, or produce food from the soil of the earth, you can and you should learn to be yourself at all times. And remember, always, what people frown upon is a phony who tries to imitate others.

Respond with one simple question when someone tries to scare you by telling you what will happen to you after death. Ask that person one simple question and stand by firmly for a reply: "How do you know?"

Learn to relate every circumstance that influences your life as something that happened for the best; for it may well be that your saddest experience will bring you your greatest assets if you will give time a chance to mellow the experience.

Divert any urge for power over others against their will—squelch that desire before it destroys you, and divert that urge to gain better control over your own mind.

Use your mind in shaping your own destiny to fit whatever purposes in life you choose, and thereby avail yourself of all the riches that come in that sealed *Rewards* envelope. Keep your mind so busy doing what you desire to do that no time will be left for your mind to stray off after what you do not want.

Express in daily prayer your gratitude for having received a multitude of blessings.

Attune your mind to attract to you the things and circumstances you desire by expressing in a daily prayer your feeling of gratitude for having received the blessings listed in that sealed envelope marked *rewards*. The prayer may be in any words or terms you choose.

Follow the habit of demanding of every day of your life a reasonable amount of dividends as you go along, instead of waiting to receive them in a future life. You may be surprised to learn that you already have the desirable things of life, although you may not have been using them.

Become a non-conformist by patterning your life and style of living to suit your physical and spiritual needs instead of copying other people. Then you will waste no time trying to keep up with the Joneses or the Smiths.

Form the habit of taking no heed from anyone unless that person is prepared to give you satisfactory evidence of the soundness of the counsel, and thus save yourself from the influence of the charlatan and the misguided.

Recognize that personal power does not come from the possession of material things alone by remembering that the late Mahatma Gandhi freed his people from the rule of the British by the simple process of following the principle of passive resistance. You, too, can keep your mind positive by refusing to accept any circumstance of which you do not approve.

Remember, as long as anyone can hurt your feelings for any cause, or make you angry against your will, there are weak spots in your mental equipment that need mending before you can express yourself through a Positive Mental Attitude.

Form the habit of tolerance and keep an open mind on all subjects, toward people of all races and creeds; learn to like people just as they are instead of demanding of them to be as you wish them to be. You have to live with people, therefore you should learn to like people and eventually you will recognize that love and affection constitute the finest of medicines for both your body and your soul. Love changes the entire chemistry of the body and conditions it for the expression of a Positive Mental Attitude. And love also extends the space you may occupy in the hearts of others. Important, also, is the fact that love is free and the best way to receive it is by giving it.

Keep a daily diary of your good deeds on behalf of others and never let the sun set on any single day without recording therein some act of human kindness. The benefits of this habit are cumulative, and will eventually give you domain over great spaces in the hearts of others. And remember, "One good deed each day will keep old man gloom away."

Give an equal benefit to others for every favor or benefit you receive. The law of increasing returns will operate in your favor and eventually, perhaps very soon, will give you the capacity to get everything you are entitled to receive. A Positive Mental Attitude must have a two-way highway on which to travel, or it will cease to function.

Avoid the fear of old age by remembering that the Creator so blessed us that nothing is ever taken away from us without something of equal or greater value being given in return. Through the operation of this profound plan, youth is replaced by wisdom. It may help you to accept and appreciate this great truth if you are reminded that the greatest achievements usually take place after they are well beyond the age of fifty, the years preceding this being merely preparatory.

Adopt the habit of advertising your achievements not by your own words, but by your deeds as expressed in behalf of the people whom you have benefitted, and let your motto be: "Deeds, not mere words."

CONDITIONING THE MIND

We are still discussing ways and means of conditioning the mind to become and remain positive. By now it must be obvious to you that the conditioning process has many facets and many methods of approach that leave no room for the alibi that the way to the establishment of a Positive Mental Attitude is unknown. Surely you will find, in this great array of steps that lead to a Positive Mental Attitude, everything you need to help you acquire this desirable asset.

Recognize the truth that there is no such circumstance as an existing personal problem with no solution. There are adequate solutions for all problems, although the best solutions of your problems may not be those you have chosen or would prefer.

Before you accept any problem as being without a solution, remember the accomplishments of Thomas A. Edison, with his handicap of only three months of schooling; or Helen Keller with her affliction of lack of sight, speech, and hearing; or Milo C. Jones with his double paralysis that deprived him of the use of his body; or Henry Ford with his limited schooling and total lack of capital plus the derision of his relatives and neighbors who believed him to be off balance mentally, because of his Definite Major Purpose which was destined to change the American way of life and create the vast Ford empire as we now know it.

Acquire the habit of welcoming friendly criticism instead of recoiling from it in a negative state of mind; get the benefit of seeing yourself and your deeds as others see them. We all need criticism, even if it comes from those whom we do not like. Criticism provides us with the opportunity to take inventory of ourselves and discover where and why we need improvements. Failure to accept and act on criticism from the public of the famous Model T automobile came near to wrecking the great Ford industrial empire. Do not fear criticism, but instead encourage it.

Profit by remembering that you will only be free if you establish the proper system for controlling and directing your thoughts.

Learn an impressive lesson on how to develop and maintain a Positive Mental Attitude, and why it pays to do so, by forming the habit of observing and analyzing those around you who live under the influence of a negative mental attitude. Would you wish to change places with any of these negative-minded people?

Free yourself from the common habit of so many people who do themselves an injustice by envying those who excel them or who appear to be more successful than they are. You can benefit by those who excel by using them as pace-makers, with a firm determination not only to catch up with them but to pass them. Then express gratitude for the influence that caused you to improve your own mental attitude.

Learn the difference between wishing, hoping, desiring, and being determined to achieve your purposes in life with a burning desire for their attainment. A burning desire is the equivalent of wishing, hoping, and desiring all rolled into one. And a burning desire can be kept active only by the aid of a Positive Mental Attitude.

Refrain from engaging in negative conversations based upon gossip, small talk, or derogatory remarks about other people; thereby keep your own mind clean and free for the expression of a Positive Mental Attitude.

BELIEVING

And now we come to a subject of paramount importance in the development and maintenance of a Positive Mental Attitude, the subject of *believing where belief is justified!* Let us review some of the circumstances calling for belief:

- Acquire an enduring belief in the existence of Infinite Intelligence; your Creator arranged for you to receive the power necessary to help you take possession of your own mind and direct it to whatever ends you may choose.

- Acquire an enduring belief in your own ability to become free and self-determining as your greatest gift from your Creator; demonstrate this belief in actions fitting its nature.

- Believe in your associates in connection with your occupation or calling in life; recognize that if they are not worthy of your complete belief, you have the wrong associates.

- And finally, believe in the power of the spoken word and see to it that you speak no word that does not harmonize in every respect with your Positive Mental Attitude.

To aid you in recognizing the importance of the spoken word, the following is an essay by Dr. Simon L. Katzoff, former medical officer, Institute for Domestic Relations, San Francisco:

The Spoken Word

The greatest mischief maker is the human tongue.
It is not what we say that counts, but how and when.
Measure your words with the yardstick
of courtesy, sentiment and gratitude.
Conversational interest is based
upon making another feel
important, and replacing telling with asking.
The less we say, the less we may
have to take back. Nature
knew her business when she gave us
two ears and only one mouth.
An unbridled tongue—even one
word thoughtlessly uttered—
may destroy the happiness of a lifetime.
To prevent faultfinding and bickering,
invite criticism, give

meritorious praise, quickly admit guilt,
and do not hesitate to say I am sorry.
Settle disputes as quickly as possible.
Every moment of delay
adds coals to the fires of dissension.

Finally, a reference table on successful conversation:

Adopt a face-to-face method.

Do not interrupt.

Be responsible.

Modulate the voice.

Omit unfavorable references to the past.

Give advice only when it is requested.

Avoid negative comparisons.

Applaud what you like and ignore what you don't.

Guard your words and your words will guard you.

These are words to remember!

It is a major indictment against the educational systems of the world that the majority of people come into the world, live their allotted span of years amidst useless struggles, and pass on without being made aware that they possess an impressive system for the usage of thought power sufficient to enable them to become free and self-determining.

And it is also a major indictment against civilization itself that the vast majority of people go all the way through life with the greater portion of their thought power centered on their fears and superstitions, and circumstances they do not want, thus attracting to themselves, by their misuse of mind power, those very circumstances.

It is also a major indictment against civilization that the greatest asset humankind ever possesses—our privilege of complete choice in controlling and directing our mind power—is not more often revealed to during the days of youth, when we are forming character by the use we make of our thought power.

Few people utilize their power to control their minds, which can resolve every problem.

The relatively few individuals who have recognized the existence of their right to control their own minds have no problems they cannot resolve through the application of this power.

I searched diligently as I read Dr. Pierre du Nouy's profound work, *Human Destiny,* to see what, if anything, he had to say with reference to this great human prerogative over the power of thought. He wrote:

> We each have our role to play individually. But, we only play it well on condition of always trying to do better, of overreaching ourselves. It is this effort which constitutes our personal participation in evolution, our duty. If we have children, we will have collaborated in a measure, modestly, statistically, *but unless we develop our personality we will have left no trace in the true, human evolution* (italics mine).

Obviously Dr. du Nouy recognized the importance of individuals exercising their privilege of choice in their thinking as a means of mental and spiritual growth, for he continues: "'An intelligent being,' said Bergson, 'carries within him the wherewithal to surpass himself. It is needful for him to know it, and it is essential for him to attempt to realize it.'"

Then Dr. du Nouy proceeds to give further evidence of his keen observations of the power of human thought. He wrote:

> The incomparable gift of the brain, with its truly amazing powers of abstraction, has rendered obsolete the slow and sometimes clumsy mechanism utilized by evolution thus far. Thanks to the brain alone, man, in the course of only three generations, has conquered the realm of air, while it took hundreds of thousands of years for animals to achieve the same result through the process of evolution.

Thanks to the brain alone, the range of our sensory organs has been increased a million fold, far beyond the fondest dreams; we have brought the moon within thirty miles of us; we see the infinitely small and we see the infinitely remote; we hear the in-audible; we have dwarfed distance and mastered physical time.

We have enslaved the forces of the universe, even before we have succeeded in understanding them thoroughly. We have put to shame the tedious and time-consuming methods of trial and error used by Nature, because Nature has finally succeeded in producing its masterpiece in the shape of the human brain. But the great laws of evolution are still active, even though adaptation has lost its importance as far as we are concerned. We are now responsible for the progress of evolution.

We are free to destroy ourselves if we misunderstand the meaning and the purpose of our victories; and we are free to forge ahead, to prolong evolution, to cooperate with God, if we perceive the meaning of it all, if we realize that it can only be achieved through a wholehearted effort toward moral and spiritual development.

Here we have a marvelous, easy-to-understand interpretation by a great scientist of the mental and physical faculties which make of man something but little less than God—but not a word concerning the ways and means by which the privilege of thinking independently may be developed until we learn how to take possession of our minds and direct them to whatever ends we choose.

Perhaps this was a mere oversight on the part of Dr. du Nouy. I had it in mind to visit him and ask for his further statements on the subject, but before I did so, he passed away.

QUESTIONS TO CONSIDER...

1. What do you think of the theory that each person born brings along into the world two sealed envelopes, one containing a list of the attainable riches by using their mind's power, and the other a list of penalties incurred if the person's mind is neglected?

2. With a Positive Mental Attitude (PMA), you can put your mind to work believing in success as your right, and your belief will guide you to it. Likewise, a negative mental attitude that believes in fear and frustration will lead you to misery and destruction. How would you rate your level of PMA? 100 percent belief in success? 50 percent? 10 percent? If not 100 percent, why not?

3. Which of the ten *rewards* listed jumped out at you as the three you most want to be rewarded with by using your PMA?

4. Which of the ten *penalties* listed jumped out at you as the three you do *not* want to be penalized with because you are not using your PMA?

5. A "burning desire" is the equivalent of wishing, hoping, and desiring all rolled into one and can be kept active only by the aid of your Positive Mental Attitude. What is your current burning desire? Are you actively fanning the flames with your PMA?

4

THE DIFFERENCE BETWEEN "WISHING" AND "BELIEVING"

The majority of people never discover the difference between wishing and believing, nor recognize that there are six steps people usually follow in using their mind power for the attainment of their desires.

These six steps are:

1. The vast majority of people go all the way through life by *merely wishing for things*. The actual percentage of people who stop at wishing is estimated at 70 percent.

2. A much smaller percentage of people *develop their wishes into desires*. These are estimated at 10 percent.

3. A still smaller percentage of people *develop their wishes and desires into hopes*. These are estimated at 8 percent.

4. A still smaller percentage of people *step up their mind power to where it becomes belief.* This percentage of the people is estimated at 6 percent.

5. And yet a very much smaller percentage of people *crystalize wishes, desires, and hopes into belief, and then into a burning desire, and finally Faith!* This percentage of the people is estimated at 4 percent.

6. And last, a very small percentage of people take the last two steps, *putting their faith into action by (1) planning and (2) acting in carrying out their plans.* This percentage is estimated at only 2 percent.

The latter class of people are the great successes in every area of endeavor.

They are the Henry Fords and the Thomas A. Edisons and the leaders in every walk of life. They are the people who recognize the power of a motivated mindset and take possession of that power and direct it to whatever ends they choose. To these people the word "impossible" has no meaning. To them everything they want or need is possible, and they manage to get it.

About 70 percent of people wish for almost everything they can imagine, but stop right there. Instead of placing their mind power on the attainment of what they desire, they allow it to dwell on the problems and difficulties they believe stand in the way of the attainment of their desires, and seem not surprised when those problems become real.

A still smaller percentage of the people carry their thinking to the third step where they hope for the fulfillment of their wishes, but do not actually believe those hopes will bring them anything tangible.

A much smaller percentage of the people, estimated at about two out of every hundred, go on through the fifth and sixth steps of using their mind power, becoming the "geniuses" in their chosen occupations, professions, and callings. These are the builders of empires, the advancers of civilization, the leaders in all callings in every nation on earth. And the only trait that differentiates them from most of the others who accept failure as their lot, is that they recognize and use their mind power for the attainment of the circumstances and things they want while the others do not.

HOW TO BECOME PART OF THE 2 PERCENT WHO ARE SUCCESSFUL

At this point I present suggestions of vital importance to those who sincerely desire to assimilate this philosophy of success and apply it in the achievement of what they desire most in life:

1. Adjust yourself to other people's state of mind and their peculiarities so as to get along peacefully with them. Refrain from taking notice of trivial circumstances in your human relations by refusing to allow

them to become controversial incidents. Big people always avoid small incidents in human relations by ignoring them as if they did not exist.

2. Establish your own technique for conditioning your mind at the start of each day so you can maintain a Positive Mental Attitude throughout the day.

3. Learn the art of selling yourself to others by indirection rather than a direct approach.

4. Adopt the habit of having a hearty laugh as a means of transmuting anger into a harmless emotion, and observe how effectively this will change the entire chemistry of your mind from negative to positive. Some master salesmen follow this habit daily as a means of conditioning their minds with a Positive Mental Attitude, which is so essential in the work of selling.

5. Express gratitude for all your adversities, failures, and defeats instead of complaining about them, then observe how quickly you will discover the seed of an equivalent benefit that comes with all such experiences.

6. Concentrate your mind on the "can do" portion of all tasks you undertake and do not worry about the "cannot do" portion unless and until it meets you face to face. By that time the "can do" portion probably will have helped you to win.

7. Learn to transmute all unpleasant circumstances into action, which calls for a Positive Mental Attitude. Make this a habit and follow it when met with every unpleasant experience.

8. Recognize that every circumstance that influences your life to any extent whatsoever is usable grist for your mill of life, and use it to pay off in some form of benefit, whether the circumstance is pleasant or unpleasant.

9. Recognize that no one can win 100 percent of the time no matter how much they may deserve to win, so learn to make allowances for the times when you will not win by transmuting the loss into some sort of gain from experience or otherwise.

10. Learn to look upon life as a continuous process of learning from experiences, both the good and the bad, and always be on alert for gains in wisdom that come a little at a time, day by day, through both the pleasant and the unpleasant experiences.

11. Remember always, every thought you release comes back greatly multiplied, to bless or curse you, so watch your thought releases and make sure you send out only those thoughts whose fruits you are willing to receive in return.

12. Be careful of your associates—other people's negative mental attitude is very contagious and rubs off a little at a time.

13. Remember that you have a dual personality; one is positive and has great capacity for belief, the other is negative and has equally great capacity for disbelief. Throw yourself on the side of the personality that believes, and the other personality will disappear for lack of exercise.

14. Remember that prayer brings the best results when the one praying has sufficient faith to see himself already in possession of what he has prayed! This calls for a Positive Mental Attitude of the highest order.

PEACE OF MIND ATTAINED ONLY WITH A POSITIVE MENTAL ATTITUDE

Peace of mind is believed by many to be the highest and most sought-after blessing that life provides. Therefore, let me enumerate some of the factors that provide this high estate:

Peace of mind is complete mastery over worry.

First of all, peace of mind is complete mastery over all forms of worry. And, peace of mind is:

- Freedom from want.
- Freedom from mental and physical ailments.
- Freedom from the superstitions of the past that have held mankind in bondage throughout the ages.
- Freedom from fear in all forms.
- Freedom from the common weakness of seeking something for nothing.
- The habit of doing your own thinking on all subjects.
- The habit of frequent self-inspection within, to determine what changes of character are needed.
- The habit of developing sufficient courage, an inherent honesty with yourself, to look at the facts of life as a realist, not as a dreamer.
- The habit of discouraging both greed and the desire to be great and powerful at the expense of others.
- The habit of helping others to help themselves.

- Recognition of the truth that the universal power of Infinite Intelligence is available to all who learn how to appropriate and use it.
- Freedom from all desire for revenge.
- Knowing who you are and what are your true virtues and abilities distinguishing you from all other people. (The you which cannot be seen in a mirror.)
- Freedom from discouragement of every nature.
- The habit of thinking in terms of what you desire.
- The habit of starting where you stand to do what your heart is set upon.
- The habit of conquering the petty misfortunes of daily occurrence instead of being mastered by them.
- The habit of looking for the seed of an equivalent benefit that comes in all adversities.
- The habit of taking life in stride, neither shrinking from the disagreeable nor over-indulging in the pleasantries.
- The joy of getting happiness from doing, rather than seeking it from possessing.
- The habit of making life pay off on your own terms, in values of your own choosing, rather than settling for a menial's hire.
- The habit of giving before trying to get.

- The habit of evaluating poverty only as a disease to be conquered and transmuted into desirable assets.

- The privilege of engaging in a labor of love of your own choice.

These are some of the joys out of which you get peace of mind by exercising a Positive Mental Attitude.

HOW A POSITIVE MENTAL ATTITUDE CAN BRING SUCCESS

Bert Cantrell, a successful industrialist at the head of a large manufacturing company, and a longtime student of my Science of Success philosophy, has given us an excellent demonstration of how a Positive Mental Attitude can bring success.

His story in his own words:

I originated a simple system which served as a check on my day to day control over my mental attitude, and served to keep me reminded that only a Positive Mental Attitude can possibly pay off in terms of success.

In a little memorandum book which I carried in my pocket I carefully recorded, in one section of the book, every circumstance under which I expressed a negative mental attitude to any degree whatsoever, including the length of time which I permitted this attitude to prevail before I switched over to the positive side of my thinking.

In another section of the book I carefully recorded every circumstance in which I acted entirely through a positive mental attitude, and when I added up the results I discovered, to my astonishment, that every form of activity in which I engaged while I was motivated by a Positive Mental Attitude led to a successful conclusion.

I also discovered that every circumstance in which I moved while under the influence of a negative mental attitude ended in disaster. In neither of these instances did the results vary. Naturally, this experiment led to my careful control of my mental attitude at all times, and within a surprisingly short time I found I had developed the habit of doing all my thinking with a Positive Mental Attitude.

This habit attracted people to me and made it easy for me to relate myself to them in a way which was beneficial to all parties concerned.

It helped me to negotiate successfully with people with whom I knew it was difficult to negotiate, and it aided me in settling many business situations harmoniously, situations which were of such a nature that only a Positive Mental Attitude could have brought success.

During my conversation with Bert Cantrell, he told me of another interesting experience he had during World War II when he was in need of an apartment at a time when rentals seemed almost impossible to obtain.

"My headquarters had been moved to Glendale, California," Bert said, "and I needed an apartment quickly. After making the rounds of many real estate offices, I reached the conclusion that I would have to rely on my own system for finding a place to live. So I inserted an advertisement in the local newspaper in which I told my story in a Positive Mental Attitude."

This is the advertisement:

> Wanted at once, by business executive and wife, an apartment in a good neighborhood and owned by a landlord who will appreciate having a tenant who will leave the apartment in better condition than he found it. References from former landlords and local business firms cheerfully given.

The advertisement brought thirteen offers of an apartment, one of which was accepted and led to a close friendship between Bert Cantrell and the owner of the apartment. And this took place when real estate people were said to have received large bonuses for the rental of houses and apartments.

The advertisement worked so successfully that a friend of Bert Cantrell who had been unable to find an apartment asked permission to use it. He published the advertisement several times and never so much as received a reply to it. And thereon hangs a tale! The friend remarked, before inserting the advertisement, "I don't think it will work for me, but I will give it a trial."

That statement was the expression of a negative mental attitude, and the results were also negative! If this were merely an isolated illustration it might be passed by as having no particular significance, but many thousands of students of mine from many parts of the world have discovered from their own experiences that a negative mental attitude has a discomforting way of bringing only negative results regardless of whether the circumstances under which it is expressed be trivial or great.

W. Clement Stone, founder and president of Combined Insurance Company of America, is one of the most outstanding examples I have ever known of what a Positive Mental Attitude can do.

During World War II, Mr. Stone took his family to Florida for a vacation, although he had been told before he made the trip

A negative mental attitude has a discomforting way of bringing only negative results regardless of the circumstances.

that it would be impossible to rent houses or apartments there. That word "impossible" only served to make him determined to demonstrate that a Positive Mental Attitude is more powerful than the negative mental attitude that readily accepts many circumstances of life as impossible.

Upon arrival in Florida, Mr. Stone interviewed several real estate firms only to be told that it was impossible to find a rental at any price. Then he took the situation into his own hands, called a taxicab and began to tour the city. In a short while, he saw a for sale sign on a large estate. He contacted the caretaker from whom he learned who owned the building and where he could be reached.

Before the day was over Mr. Stone had sold the owner the idea that the house would be more saleable if someone were living in it who could show it at any hour, and that night he and his family occupied one of the finest and best furnished houses in the city, at a very nominal rental. Moreover, they were told they could keep the house as long as they desired to remain in Florida.

THE POWER OF PMA

That is but one of many examples through which W. Clement Stone has revealed the secret of his astounding business and financial achievements by the application of a Positive Mental Attitude.

He travels often by airplane and often his secretaries try, without success, to get desired reservations for him, but I have observed that this never disturbs him at all. He simply packs his baggage, makes his appearance at the airport a few minutes ahead of the departure of his plane, and strangely enough, he nearly always finds a way to get a seat on the plane.

If this happened only occasionally one might properly attribute it to mere chance, but it is the rule and not the exception. Those who are closest to Mr. Stone recognize that his own controlled and directed Positive Mental Attitude works for him in connection with all the circumstances that influence his life, financially and otherwise.

Now I shall present another example of an astounding achievement based on a Positive Mental Attitude. The principal in this case is William C. Robinson, president and majority owner of a large lumber and building supplies company in Paris, Missouri.

While Mr. Robinson was still a very young man, he left the family farm and procured a job at a lumber yard in Paris as a laborer, unloading cars and the like, at very small wages. Shortly after he got this job he procured a copy of one of my books from which he got the necessary inspiration to start working on the attainment of a Definite Major Purpose, a partnership in the lumber yard where he worked. By applying my Science of Success philosophy, Mr. Robinson had no difficulty in buying his way into the business with promissory notes, which he soon paid off, giving him a controlling interest in the business.

Inspired by the swiftness with which he had lifted himself from day laborer to control of a growing and profitable business, Mr. Robinson organized a local group of the top ranking men and women of his community into a study class based on the Science of Success, and named it Club Success Unlimited.

The Club consisted of 97 members, all of whom embraced and applied the Science of Success philosophy so enthusiastically that sudden improvements in their financial status began to become evident, and elderly people who observed these rapid changes said that nothing had come to that community within the previous 50 years that had so profoundly improved the thinking habits and the financial conditions of the people, including in many instances those who did not belong to Mr. Robinson's Club Success Unlimited.

From an average farming community, the town of Paris, Missouri, and from some six or more nearby towns and communities, the members of Club Success Unlimited blossomed out into a brand-new world of their own making, a world in which the people began expressing a Positive Mental Attitude.

Merchants in Paris, Missouri, began improving their storefronts in keeping with the changed thinking that began with Mr. Robinson's Club Success Unlimited, and some of them erected new and more modern buildings than any the town had known before. For examples:

- A local physician who was a member of the Club erected a brand-new medical clinic that would be a credit to any city.

- A dealer in plumbing and heating equipment built a brand-new store and equipped it with a stock of merchandise that could not be excelled in many large cities.

- A local minister began preaching sermons based on the principles of the Science of Success, with the result that for the first time during the church's existence all the pews were filled to an overflow capacity, and the finances of the church were so improved that some much needed repairs were made, including a new roof and improvement of the acoustics.

- A local school teacher who was a member of the Club was inspired to begin a business during her off hours, from which she soon began to earn much more than she received as a teacher.

- The Mark Twain Cafe, where the Club held its meetings, grew so rapidly it became a figurative "gold mine" and enabled the owner to buy the building outright.

And should you go to the little town of Paris, Missouri, today, you would find the atmosphere permeated with a Positive Mental Attitude on the part of a majority of the people, all due to the fact that William C. Robinson became indoctrinated with the Science of Success philosophy and its emphasis on a Positive Mental Attitude and passed them on to others who, like himself, embraced them and discovered that they could give them changed lives!

I could provide many more examples of the results of adopting a Positive Mental Attitude. Please apply what you have learned and you, too, will attain and benefit from a Positive Mental Attitude and motivated mindset.

QUESTIONS TO CONSIDER...

1. Think about your normal, usual attitude. Then write your definition of a PMA that you want to absorb into your daily lifestyle.

2. Of the six steps people usually follow in using their mind power to achieve their desires, right now, where do you fit into the percentage scale? Are you with the 70 percent, 10 percent, 8 percent, 6 percent, 4 percent, or 2 percent? Where would you rather be?

3. From the list of what peace of mind means, which five are the most attractive to you? Are you willing to adopt a PMA to attain those five, today?

4. Do you have as much faith in your Positive Mental Attitude as Mr. Cantrell did when he wrote that ad for an apartment? What issue or problem are you facing today that can be turned around with faith in your PMA?

5. Mr. Stone exhibited faith in his PMA to get seats on planes as well as in other circumstances. Are his examples enough to make you a believer rather than a wisher?

5

APPLIED FAITH

The other day a man told me a story I would like to pass on to you. He was driving from Los Angeles to Palm Springs in California and was rolling along fine until his car stopped dead. He repeatedly tried the starter, but not a cylinder would fire. Being a businessman and not a mechanic, he didn't know the first thing about the workings of his car. He got out, however, lifted the hood, and looked in rapt amazement and some confusion at the array of gadgets that greeted his eyes. Angered by his own mechanical ignorance, he slammed down the hood, locked the car, and started walking down the highway to find a garage.

He trudged along for nearly three miles in the hot desert sun and arrived at a garage by the roadside in a good sweat. He rode back to his car with the mechanic. When the mechanic lifted the hood, he loosened a nut on the side of the carburetor, took out a tiny screen, held it up to the sunlight and, after a glance, gave it a quick blow with his breath. He shook it a few times and put it back in. The engine immediately responded to the starter.

The mechanic explained that all that was wrong with the engine was that the flow of its life giving fluid–gasoline–had been temporarily shut off by the dust that had collected on the little screen. Being somewhat of a philosopher, the mechanic made the observation that men are like that–sometimes their screens get clogged and they fail to accept the bounteous blessings that a generous Providence has provided for them.

This caused my friend to do some thinking. He had just received a tremendous lesson in Applied Faith. He realized how many unhappy situations in life are caused by some interruptions of the inflowing life energy from Infinite Intelligence. He understood clearer than ever before how the clogged screen of doubt, fear, and worry could shut off the "gas," which is forever flowing around us.

This simple story brings us face to face with the matter of Applied Faith.

AN APPROACH TO FAITH

In approaching this subject, I feel keenly the responsibility I have assumed in attempting to lay before you a practicable, working technique for taking possession of the power of your own mind, and for relating your inner self harmoniously to the great cosmic forces of the universe in which you live.

I am going to do my best to tell you what Faith really is, explain the source of its power, and give you a simple method you may adopt and make it effective in your life. When you understand Applied Faith, you will have taken a long step forward toward achieving your objectives.

Let me say at the outset that I use the word "applied" in connection with the word "faith," to distinguish it unmistakably from any sort of religious connotation. It is not my purpose to encroach the slightest on the field of the clerics and other gentlemen of the cloth. The Faith I am talking about is applied to the achievement of a Definite Major Purpose in life. Hence the term Applied Faith.

You've probably heard and read a lot of different definitions of faith, and some of them have appealed to you more than others. I dare say that there are as many definitions of faith as there are persons who have seriously contemplated the great universe in which we find ourselves, and who have figured out a plausible explanation of the elements of our environment, which gives them the courage to face life with chin up, eyes bright, and a smile on their faces.

The purpose of this chapter is to describe the exact meaning of Faith, with suggestions for its application to the solving of your daily problems. I am talking about the active, motivating Faith that you can put into daily practice, without regard to any form of theology or religion. The only religion I intend to deal with is the broad, general religion of right thinking and right living as you meet the important human relationships in the real situations of life.

I am not going to content myself with merely telling you to *have faith*. People have been saying that to each other since the birth of civilization, but very few have gone on to explain *how you may get faith* and use it in the solution of life's problems. I am going to sincerely attempt to be different in this respect, by telling you all that my more than 40 years of experience in dealing with the minds of other men, and with the unfolding of my own mind, have taught me about ways and means of acquiring and using faith. Of course if I fall short of this goal, it will be because I have done my best and it was not good enough.

In all fairness to all of us, I feel that I should tell you that you must use your own mind and reach your own conclusions on this most profound subject. And if I succeed only in inspiring you to serious thought and deep meditation on the subject of Faith, I will have rendered you a service of great value. For an understanding of Faith, you have to become acquainted with the inner workings of your own mind.

To understand faith, you have to be acquainted with your mind's inner workings.

The real difficulty in defining Faith is that it is a state of mind. And not a passive state of mind at that, where the mind is merely giving assent, but an *active* state of mind. The mind is in the state of relating itself to the great eternal *elan vital* (vital force) of the universe. You see, the word "faith" is what is known as an abstract idea, or a purely mental conception, and that is why it is not better understood.

The only way it can be understood is to see someone or something real or tangible or concrete doing something or expressing something. The real, tangible thing in the case of Faith is using our mind to understand the powers that surround us in this wonderful world, and trying to harmonize life with those thrilling powers as we feel them.

Such a relationship—that is, the relationship between the human mind and the unseen powers of the universe—is infinite in its possibilities, and therein lies the difficulty of saying exactly what Faith is. Our language is hopelessly inadequate to describe or delineate infinity, but it is possible to point out how Faith works, as it has been demonstrated in the lives of men and women of achievement. These examples, illustrations and ideas will serve as stimuli for your own mind to commence its search for this unlimited power.

Thus, we must describe what Faith *does, or causes us to do,* rather than to try to penetrate the essence of it. In final analysis, Faith is the activity of individual minds "finding themselves" and establishing a working association with the power variously referred to as the "universal mind," the "great unseen," "divine mind," or by the more orthodox religionists as "God," and by the students of this philosophy as "Infinite Intelligence."

AN EXPLANATION OF INFINITE INTELLIGENCE

I wish at this point to explain just what I mean by the term Infinite Intelligence, because it is my opinion that no one may ever reach the state of mind called Faith without a positive, definite belief in a Supreme Being.

In arriving at this belief and conviction, you may employ every faculty you possess. Observation, experimentation, feeling, prayer, meditation, and thought are all legitimate approaches. In all other activities you use your natural gifts, the senses of body and "spirit," and the power of mind, to organize information and knowledge; and so in this case, all methods by which facts are discovered may be used in establishing your contact with this supreme power.

Humans learn primarily by seeing the effects or by accepting the statements of trusted others. In the search for the Infinite Power behind all creation, you may properly look for evidence in the external universe that lies beyond the borders of your own body; you may look to your own inner self by exploring as best you can the workings of your own mind; and you may examine the accumulated history of civilization.

The external universe has always been, to thinkers, evidence of the existence of a Supreme, Creative, Directing Power. Centuries ago, David, the shepherd boy, sang, "The heavens declare the glory of God; and the firmament showeth his handiwork."

The heavens today still remain the sublime object of our investigation and speculation; they are indeed witnesses of some great power at work. The advance of science reveals many secrets of the working of this power we call Nature. Every process of Nature is orderly. No chance, disorder, or chaos has been seen in the physical universe. The sun does not rise in the East today and in the West tomorrow. All of the phenomena of Nature are products of law; not a single exception has thus far been found.

The universe exists under a reign of perfect law. Such prevalent order, such obedience to law, clearly implies intelligent planning and Definiteness of Purpose. Order is the product of intelligent direction. Sober men of science today declare that the universe appears as the product of thought! The conclusion is inescapable. There can be no planning or purpose without a mind; there can be no thought without a thinker. The universe declares that there is intelligent purpose in nature and that, therefore, there must be a supreme Infinite Intelligence directing it.

> The sun, the moon, the stars, the seas, the hills and
> the plains. Are not these, O Soul, the Vision of Him
> who reigns? –Lord Tennyson

Take a look at any wristwatch. You know who made it; you can learn how it operates; you can analyze the metal of its parts. You know also that your watch did not come into existence without the aid of organized intelligence, and you know that the particular intelligence in this case is the human mind. Equally well, you know that the intelligence the person used did not originate in his mind, but that he was merely an instrumentality expressing the creative force of a greater intelligence.

If you take the watch apart, separating the parts from their correct working relationship to each other, and put them in a hat and shake them, never in a million years would they, nor could they, re-assemble themselves into the smoothly functioning machine called a watch. Your watch operates accurately only because there is organized intelligence and a definite plan behind it. It is not unreasonable, therefore, to have Faith that there is an organized Infinite Intelligence behind the operation of the universe that our senses describe to us.

You can see Infinite Intelligence operating in the miracle of reproduction. Two tiny specks of protoplasm combining and bringing into being the marvelous chemical, mechanical, electrical, spiritual machine we know as a human life. Those two small particles form the nucleus that attracts energy, matter, and intelligence sufficient to reproduce the genetic inheritances for unnumbered generations.

You can see it in the mystery by which an acorn and a handful of soil produce an oak tree. It may be seen in the matchless engineering and functional design by which the tree is attached to the ground so as to successfully defy the fury of storms and winds, and how it draws its sustenance while remaining immovable in its original position in the earth.

The very food we eat and the fabrics we wear originate as some unexplained reaction between the light of the sun and the air, and the water and earth of our planet. All forms of vegetation live by the process of photosynthesis, or "light building up," which we do not now understand. The delicately balanced chemical equations necessary for this truly wonderful process speaks with eloquence the work of an Intelligence that is indeed beyond our understanding.

APPLIED FAITH DEFINITION

This is the definition of Faith that I like better than any I have yet seen or heard: "*Faith* is a state of mind which you may develop by conditioning your mind to receive Infinite Intelligence. *Applied Faith* is adapting the power received from Infinite Intelligence to a Definite Major Purpose."

Your mind differs from all others. Your reactions to the experiences of life are different from everyone else's. Therefore, the exact process that clears your mind of all negative thoughts and prepares it for the inflow of Infinite Intelligence and acquire Faith, is for you to determine for yourself. I offer suggestions throughout this book that can assist you in working out the particular technique adapted to your personality.

Applied Faith has been called the "dynamo of the entire philosophy," because Applied Faith gives you the power to put the philosophy into action. The word "dynamo," is just another name for a generator of electric power. Faith is the state of mind in which you contact the power of Infinite Intelligence and focus it upon the object of your desire.

Faith is a state of mind where you temporarily relax your reason and willpower and open your mind completely to the guidance of Infinite Intelligence for the attainment of some definite purpose. The guidance comes in the form of an idea or a plan that comes to you while you are in this receptive attitude.

Our mind is the only thing the Creator gave us the complete right of control. Surely this fact conveys the suggestion that the Creator considered this right the greatest asset given to humans. It also leaves no doubt the Creator intended us to assume the responsibility of exercising that right and using it to further our purposes on earth, thereby possibly cooperating with Him in the fulfillment of *His* ultimate purposes, whatever they may be.

Infinite Intelligence recognizes no limitations except those we impose upon ourselves.

The mind has been cleverly provided with an approach to Infinite Intelligence through our subconscious. The subconscious mind, according to the best evidence available, is the gateway between the conscious human mind and the vast reservoir of Infinite Intelligence. It might be likened unto a "spigot" or "valve" through which flows the stream of intelligence that we are dependent on for our growth and development and the unfolding of our innate powers. In this inflowing stream of intelligence "we live, and move, and have our being," so says the Good Book.

We must, therefore, keep this gateway open. We must keep it free from self-imposed limitations and restrictions. We must do nothing to dam up this inflowing energy. Infinite Intelligence recognizes no limitations except those we impose upon ourselves.

Our mind is an instrument for receiving and distributing power of Infinite Intelligence, which is basic to understanding Applied Faith.

At least one human purpose here on earth seems to be to act as the receiver and distributor of the power of Infinite Intelligence. To the extent that we cooperate in this purpose, we ally ourselves with the forces behind all nature. And conversely, to the extent that we look out only for our own selfish ends, we are opposing this power, or hindering its flow.

The power of Infinite Intelligence pours life into us as a flowing stream, maintaining all of the functions of our bodies and minds, and we can use it to guide and govern the circumstances and conditions of our lives, *if* we act as conductors of this energy and shape it according to our constructive purposes.

Whatever the mind conceives, we can achieve—if it doesn't run counter to natural laws, and is in harmony with a moral and orderly universe.

This inflowing power has no limitations or defects; it is forced to manifest itself in this world in a way we, as individuals, can understand and express it.

Life energy flows into a positive, receptive mind in a continuous stream, just as strips of aluminum alloy are fed into the punch presses of a fabricating plant. Going in it is potential life, potential abundance, potential power, potential riches. But like the aluminum strips, *coming out* the formed parts can be only what we have expressed—what the "stamping machines" of our own convictions and beliefs have impressed upon the original material.

Whatever we accept, whatever we love, cherish, or desire with a burning desire and hold constantly in our thoughts as our own, finds fulfillment in our lives. As sunlight passing through a prism is broken up into its component color rays, so Infinite Intelligence in passing through our conscious minds takes on a variety of delightful forms.

The "prism" of our minds can be darkened by the imperfections of our own creations of worry and fear and failure consciousness, until it shuts out all the lighter, happier colors. It is a perfect stream of intelligence that starts through us, but just as a poorly made die in the punch press can cut crude and ugly pieces from the best of raw material and a faulty prism can turn beams of sunshine into shadows, so can our disbeliefs and doubts turn perfect life energy into sickness, poverty, discord, and misery.

The first essential then, is to be careful of the pattern of the die–watch your desires and your beliefs in them as carefully as the director of the U.S. Mint watches the die that casts the silver coins it turns out. Instead of picturing what you fear and do not want that stamps that impression into your mind, be sure to instead picture the conditions you want–trust, confidence, joy.

What do you want? Make up your mind precisely what it is you want, through Definiteness of Purpose. Then apply the power of your Faith to it. Like the perfect flower that lies latent in the unopened bud, the seed of your burning desire needs only the sunshine of your Faith to start germinating.

You acquire this power of Faith by utilizing the instrument of contact with Infinite Intelligence, which is your subconscious mind. You activate your subconscious mind and get it busy

Faith entails keeping your mind on what you want and off what you don't want!

focusing this Infinite Power on the accomplishment of your purposes by continually bombarding it with a clear-cut statement of those purposes *while you are in a state of high emotion.*

Here's a tremendous idea for you to think over: the creative force of the entire universe functions through your mind when you establish a Definite Purpose and apply Faith to its fulfillment!

The one sure, infallible way to separate yourself from the mess of humanity and climb out of the level of "average" and mediocrity is not to journey to some desert or forgotten island, nor lock yourself in solitary confinement, but to hitch your wagon to the star of some strong purpose. In this way you pull yourself out of the mass of self-centered, self-seeking, negative humanity and ally yourself with the great life-giving power of Infinite Intelligence!

Faith in Infinite Intelligence is something you must acquire for yourself and the only way to do this is by examining closely the visible evidences of the existence of Infinite Intelligence as they appear in the known familiar realities of the physical world about us. Then apply to this evidence the power of your analysis, meditation, and thought.

SILENT MEDITATION

I cannot overemphasize the importance of *silent meditation.* This form of concentrated thinking activates the subconscious mind and accelerates or speeds up its receptive capability to more efficiently establish contact between your conscious mind and Infinite Intelligence. This is the way to take possession of your mind and tap this inexhaustible source of power.

You should set a definite period of not less than one hour out of every twenty-four to engage in deep, serious thought about your relationship with Infinite Intelligence. You will find that this investment of time will pay you dividends that enrich your life beyond your present dreams. If you happen to be a religious person, you can make this a period of prayer. During this time, you may receive a slightly different idea of prayer than is held by the average individual.

From what I have said, it must be obvious to you that Faith is a state of mind you can attain only by properly conditioning your mind, clearing it of all negative thoughts of want, poverty, fear, ill health, and disharmony. When you have cleared your mind of these negative thoughts, there are three easy steps you must take to create the state of mind known as Faith:

1. Express a definite desire for the achievement of a purpose and relate it to one or more of the basic motives.

2. Create a definite and specific plan to attain that desire.

3. Start acting on that plan, putting every conscious effort behind it.

These three steps will take you as far as you can go alone. From that point on, your subconscious mind will have to carry the plans to their logical conclusions. However, since Infinite Intelligence is available through the subconscious, if there are better and more perfect plans, you will be inspired by a "hunch" or "intuition" to change the plans you have made.

This procedure places your spiritual strength squarely back of your desire and hands the problem over to your Creator! When the solution to your problem comes, *as it surely will if you rely* on your Faith in the Infinite, it will come as an idea or plan transmitted to your conscious mind by the subconscious, which is the doorway to Infinite power, as explained.

Never mind what your reason tells you about this mode of procedure. In conditioning your mind to receive Infinite Intelligence to guide you, you have temporarily subdued your faculty of reason. This part of the instruction is very important. Unless you can willingly follow that guidance, your reason will challenge you at every step and you will not relax your will and submit yourself entirely to the higher power you are seeking. You will need some practice to acquire this art of conditioning your mind to be receptive.

You may wonder how you will know when you have an answer. You will come to recognize the soundness of the plan and the authenticity of its power by the feeling of intense enthusiasm that accompanies its inspiration. When the plan comes through to your conscious mind, accept it with appreciation and gratitude and act on it at once. Do not hesitate, argue, challenge, worry, fret about it, or wonder if it's right. Act on it!

Remember, it is not your responsibility, nor anyone else's, to demand of Infinite Intelligence an explanation of how or why it works. You have done your part when you have followed these instructions.

Here, a further word about prayer. If you make your prayers an expression of gratitude and thanksgiving for the *blessings you already have received*, instead of complaining about what you do not have, you will obtain results a great deal faster.

Faith cannot fail if you open your mind completely for guidance!

If your plans do not mature when you expect them to, repeat the procedure I have outlined until you do get results. You may be confident that if your purpose is right and worthy–not calculated to harm, destroy, or contrary to the known laws of Nature–your Faith cannot fail. To question this is the same as questioning the power of your Creator. The working principle of Faith is as definite and as precise as the power that holds the stars and planets in their fixed courses. Faith cannot fail if you open your mind completely for guidance!

Our doubts are traitors and make us lose the good we oft might win, by fearing to attempt. –Shakespeare

TAKE ACTION

In carrying out the instructions in this chapter, be willing to do your part. Make up your mind what you want, organize a plan for attaining it, then put the plan into action. If you receive inspiration to change or modify your plan, adopt the new one immediately. Infinite Intelligence may give you plans far better than those you create yourself. You will intuitively recognize the superiority of the new plan when it comes.

Do not expect Infinite Intelligence to bring you the physical equivalent of your desire! Accept with gratitude a plan that you can fulfill your desires through using the usual rules of human conduct. Do not look for miracles. Infinite Intelligence prefers to work through natural laws, employing whatever physical means available.

Do not expect something for nothing. Nature frowns on "bargains." You must give an equivalent value for the object of your desire. Anything you happen to acquire through selfish or unethical practices will have no enduring value.

Examine your motives and desires carefully to be sure that they include no injustices to others. Unjust motives will set up a counter force of opposition that may be far stronger than your desire. Be sure that your desires tend toward giving and good.

It is hard to make a snowball by pushing it up the hill, counter to the natural law of life. If you try you will find that it will become bigger than you are; it will get out of control and come crashing down the mountainside on your own head. Every seed brings forth after its own kind. Be sure to include in the seed of your desire some love for others, some of the milk of human kindness.

Remember:
The milk of human
kindness will never
be rationed.

Once you have glimpsed the possibilities of the actual service your mind performs, you will never again lack the self-reliance to draw upon the forces available to you, through your mind, for every need of life. You will have no difficulty in opening your mind, at will, for the guidance of Infinite Intelligence when you face problems that seem temporarily beyond solution by your own reason.

Strangely enough, with all this power available, the majority of people permit themselves to be filled with fears that exist only in their imaginations. *The worst enemy of mankind is fear.*

You can't exercise the pure, clean power of Faith, which is Infinite Intelligence expressing itself in your life, as long as there is one iota of fear or worry in your mind about anything. You have to learn to give your mind a mental bath and, no matter what the price is, go through with it.

That's the first step in conditioning your mind for Faith—get rid of what is causing you to be afraid and take action to fulfill your desires.

Faith and fear cannot exist in the heart at the same time.

QUESTIONS TO CONSIDER...

1. Have you come to realize that many unhappy situations in life are caused by interruptions of the life energy flow from Infinite Intelligence? Is the flow clogged with doubt, fear, and worry?

2. What is the state of your Faith? Strong? Mediocre? Weak? How easy is it for you to temporarily relax your reason and willpower and open your mind completely to the guidance of Infinite Intelligence to achieve some definite purpose?

3. How serious are you about taking time every day for silent meditation and/or prayer? What advantages could this have in your life? What disadvantages?

4. Do you often expect something for nothing? Or, do you routinely give an equivalent value for the object of your desire? Give several examples.

5. Have you examined your motives and desires lately to ensure they include no injustices to others? Are you sure your desires tend toward giving and good, rather than selfishness and negativity?

QUESTIONS TO CONSIDER...

CONQUERING YOUR FEARS

Nearly everybody in the world suffers from one or more of the following seven basic fears, and some people suffer from all of them. Fear prevents you from creating a motivated mindset. The most common, basic fears include:

1. Poverty

2. Criticism

3. Ill health

4. Loss of love

5. Old age

6. Loss of liberty

7. Death

Because you must drive out the negative influences before the positive power of Faith can enter your mind, we now examine these basic fears that you must master.

FIRST BASIC FEAR—THE FEAR OF POVERTY

The fear of poverty is the most destructive of the seven basic fears. It heads the list because it is the most difficult to master. Nothing brings people so much suffering and humiliation as poverty! Only those who have experienced poverty understand the full meaning of this. It is really no wonder that we fear poverty. If someone has money, few of us stop to ask how he acquired it. He virtually makes his own laws; he is the invisible power behind the political scene; he establishes business policy; and nearly everyone around him bows low in respect at his presence.

In back of the fear of poverty often lies the worst indictment of a person's dealings with others. Through bitter experience most of us have learned that some people are not trustworthy when it comes to money matters. If you search the statute books you will see that a great majority of all laws have been enacted for the purpose of safeguarding one person from another in dealings with property.

It will behoove those who resent poverty and are determined to get out of it, to analyze yourselves most completely for signs of this fear, then fasten your minds on a positive substitute for each of the negatives that bind your habit.

Major Symptoms

To aid you in your personal search within yourself, some suggestions of the major symptoms of a fear of poverty are given here:

- *Lack of Ambition* is shown by accepting whatever life "hands out" without challenging it–general mental and physical laziness.

- *Failure to Make Decisions* permits someone else to make up your mind for you, thus surrendering your most precious prerogative and divine gift and privilege of controlling your own thoughts, making your own decisions, and taking advantage of the blessings of American liberty to become self-determining.

- *Making Excuses* for your failure; offering alibis as to why others have passed you in the economic race; envying and criticizing the success of others.

- *Lack of Self-Control;* living beyond one's means; intemperance in personal habits; general lack of poise and self-control; wearing a frown or scowl.

- *Negative Mental Attitude* is the habit of expecting failure instead of concentrating on ways to succeed; knowing all the reasons why something won't work instead of the reasons why it must and will work; having failures instead of successes for your heroes; keeping your eye on the hole instead of the doughnut; general pessimism.

- *Procrastinating* Is the habit some people have of never doing today what can be put off until tomorrow; refusal or dodging responsibility; planning what to do if you fail instead of concentrating on success; expecting and accepting poverty instead of demanding and receiving riches.

For emphasis, let me repeat here that fear of poverty, like all other fears, is a state of mind–and only you have the power to control your state of mind. You are the one who decides to tolerate the fear of poverty and permit it to rob you of initiative, imagination, and enthusiasm; and you are the one who limits your self-expression and prevents your enjoyment of the riches of life.

Know this–you can substitute a positive mental attitude any time you wish. And you may be sure of one thing–until you get that fear of poverty out of your consciousness, you are not going to get ahead in life. You will not understand this philosophy or anything else worthwhile beyond mere existence. You have it within your power to acquire a "success consciousness," which will prove the perfect antidote for the poison of the fear of poverty.

Demand much! Set a high goal! Go for it!

Definiteness of Purpose is the beginning of a success consciousness. Find out what it is you want from life and look for it all the time. Demand much! Set a high goal and go after it. I quote here a poem by Jessie B. Rittenhouse which you will do well to commit to memory:

> I bargained with Life for a penny
> And Life would pay no more;
> However, I begged at evening
> When I counted my scanty store.
> For Life is a just employer;
> He gives you whatever you ask,
> But once you have set the wages,
> Why, you must bear the task.
> I worked for a menial's hire,
> Only to learn dismayed,
> That any wage I had asked of Life,
> Life would have willingly paid.

Successful people do not bargain with Life for poverty! They know that there is a power through which Life may be made to pay off on their own terms. They know that this power is available to everyone who comes into possession of their own mind! Carve out a career; don't just bore your way through life!

As Andrew Carnegie said, "The man who acquires the ability to take full possession of his own mind may take possession of everything else to which he is justly entitled."

SECOND BASIC FEAR—FEAR OF CRITICISM

My, oh my, what criticism does to people! I shall consider the effects of this fear under two divisions: *first,* those of a petty and trivial nature, and *second,* those of a serious nature.

Clothing fashions and consumer trends are evidence of *trivial fears of criticism.* As a matter of fact, if the clothing manufacturers didn't capitalize on this very common form of fear of criticism, there wouldn't be such emphasis on "style." The manufacturer changes the shape of pieces of apparel, gets some of the well-to-do group to wear the new creations, and immediately all over the nation women and men flock to the stores to get the "latest," thus accomplishing the purposes of the manufacturer in the first place—sell more clothes and make more money.

The makers of other necessities, conveniences, and gadgets capitalize on this fear of criticism, too. New automobiles are sold every year to people whose cars are nowhere near worn out; wristwatches, costume jewelry, refrigerators, washing machines, toasters, almost everything you can think of undergoes constant change in an effort to capture the dollars of those fearful of what their neighbors will say. I'm not saying that this is all bad, because every once in a while some improvement is made that actually enhances the efficiency of the device.

Now for the more *serious aspects of this fear of criticism.* Fear of what people will say or think keeps many from developing and presenting ideas that could give them independence if they would only act on their own initiative. This fear of criticism sometimes assumes the shape of a demon from hell who sits on the shoulder of someone who could achieve and whispers: "Don't do that! What would people think?!" In this way, fear of criticism robs people of their initiative, destroys their creative ability, restricts their individuality, and tends to stereotype them a conformist. Fear of being criticized undermines some people's self-reliance and they tend to develop an inferiority complex.

Parents–with good intentions but a poor understanding of psychology–often do their children irreparable injury by criticizing them, shaming them, or making fun of them and their childhood dreams of achievement. Teasing an adolescent boy about his "girlfriends" is one definitely dangerous practice that can lead to permanent social maladjustment in the case of sensitive personalities.

Strangely enough, criticism is one form of service that nearly everyone is willing to render willingly, and usually without

The only place someone can work and hope to get flowers for mistakes–is in a dynamite factory.

charge or even an invitation. It is one type of service nearly everyone is very generous to dole out.

It is important to realize the significant difference between criticism and constructive suggestion. Oftentimes an employee, an associate, or a child needs correction regarding habits that are not productive, are wasteful, or in bad taste. A well-balanced person will learn to accept a constructive suggestion and will learn not to brood over past mistakes.

Self-Analysis Regarding Criticism

The following are some headings to guide your self-analysis of your ability to stand up under criticism. See if you suffer from this fear that is so enervating to so many people.

- *Keeping Up with the Joneses:* Trying to maintain a "front" in competition with neighbors, which often requires spending beyond your income.

- *Bragging:* The habit of bragging about your achievements, either real or imaginary. Strangely, it often happens that people cover up their real feelings of inferiority by boasting, using "big words," and minimizing others who are successful, to give an impression of superiority.

- *Embarrassment:* Inability to express definite decisions; nervous fear of meeting people; lack of self-confidence; reticence; fear of those of superior authority; avoidance of responsibility; lack of personal initiative.

The fear of criticism is almost as common as the fear of poverty and, similarly, it saps initiative and prevents the full play of the imagination, thus undermining two essential ingredients of personal achievement.

THIRD BASIC FEAR—FEAR OF ILL HEALTH

This fear is related to another fear that comes later in the list, the fear of death. Sometimes ill health brings near death, and so the social and physical heredity of a person tends to develop this fear. Social heredity is the habits of thinking and acting in accordance with "customs" or social patterns of behavior, which a person falls heir to by reason of membership in a particular culture. The physical heredity, of course, is the actual physical body we receive from our parents, with whatever inherent weaknesses and tendencies toward disease it may have.

As a matter of social heredity, humankind has had painted for himself such terrifying pictures of "other worlds" to which he may be consigned at death, that it is no wonder a majority of people are afraid of anything that may hasten the journey. This fear is probably related also to the desire of self-preservation. Regardless of its exact origin, it is a very prevalent fear.

The patent medicine manufacturers capitalize on this fear to sell their nostrums and panaceas. One of the symptoms of this fear is the willingness to try anything anybody suggests as possibly helpful to their "condition." There is evidence, too, that some unethical members of the healing arts like to keep alive this fear of ill health, as it tends to fill their coffers with much bounty.

I am by no means saying that there are not cases where patients need the structure of their bodies worked over mechanically, such as where a bone is broken, or where a foreign object enters the system, and surgery is required. Then again, sometimes the chemistry of the digestive system is out of kilter and needs some balancing, and there are times when the dentist needs to pull out a decayed tooth.

However, a study I made a few years ago among doctors in all the fields of therapy showed that 75 percent of people who go to doctors' offices are suffering from nothing more serious than hypochondria. That is a five dollar word that means imaginary illness. Some doctors love this.

There is overwhelming evidence that a disease can originate as a negative thought that the person continues to "sell" himself or herself through auto-suggestion, until the physical symptoms actually appear. Most medical doctors now agree that there is a definite relation between the patient's mental attitude and the physical condition. Realizing this truth, then it is equally true that maintaining a positive mental attitude and developing sound "health consciousness" whereby you expect, demand, and receive health-sustaining elements from the nutrients of your food, the fresh air, and sunshine can guarantee you sound physical health!

Self-Analysis Regarding Ill Health

The following are a few suggestions for your self-analysis of this fear of ill health:

- *The Drug Store Habit.* Do you realize that of all God's creatures, humans are the only ones who have developed drug stores, and that there is a definite relationship between this fact and the fact that people suffer more diseases than all other creatures put together? Examine your habits to see if you listen to all of the radio and television ads and advice of well-meaning friends and then go to the drug store, thinking (by what logic, I know not) that you will get good health out of a bottle. Let me warn you that good health does *not* come in bottles!

- *Self-Pity.* This is the habit of feeling sorry for yourself, often used as an excuse for plain old laziness and as an alibi for lack of ambition.

- *Drinking Alcohol.* Aside from the negative moral side of this habit, intemperance in drinking alcoholic beverages–to cover up physical, mental, or emotional pains–will definitely not promote sound health. Rather, the cause of the pain should be sought out and removed.

FOURTH BASIC FEAR—FEAR OF THE LOSS OF LOVE

This fear stems from the tremendous competition that goes on in the selection of a mate. It is the fear that forms dementia praecox, known as jealousy. This fear can be the most dangerous of all the fears, as it sometimes leads to a permanent mental unbalance. It is also a very costly fear, if the fear is realized. If you don't think the fear of the loss of love causes a lot of trouble, you have not read the news of late. Social students are alarmed about the effect our present divorce rate is apt to have on the general moral structure of our homes and our nation. But I see no reason why anyone should be afraid of the loss of love. The affectionate response between man and woman, which is the type of love one most fears losing, is one of the great wonders in the world, but I personally don't believe it is worth sacrificing a lifetime to retain.

This fear is so intimate, and the symptoms are so generally well understood, I feel it is unnecessary to elaborate further, other than to say that one of the more dangerous symptoms of this fear is that of taking unusually hazardous chances to provide extra money to indulge the whims of the one whose love you fear losing. I know of an otherwise honest man who went to prison for income tax evasion. His only defense, and it obviously was not good enough, was that he needed the extra money to favor his wife, whose standard of living he was otherwise unable to maintain. This is what I mean by sacrificing too much to free oneself from this fear of the loss of love.

FIFTH BASIC FEAR—FEAR OF OLD AGE

This is one of the fears I like to jump on with both feet. I like to laugh about this fear, because it is a whole lot better to laugh about it than to cry about it; and if you will remember to laugh about it, you will be far better off. I discovered some time ago that when I had a birthday, the proper thing to do was to take a year *off* my age instead of adding one. Implementing this idea, I began to feel younger, and I really and truly believe I began to change in appearance so that I even looked younger, simply because I sold myself on the idea of youth rather than old age.

I made a survey of the outstanding men of the world down through the ages and I discovered that the men of greatest achievement in life started their best work after 55, and some did their best work after 60 and 70. The reason for that is that, with age, nature compensates you for the loss of youth with one of the greatest things in the whole world—wisdom. Wisdom comes from experience.

I had a mighty good time when I was 20, 25, and 30, but I wouldn't want to go back to those ages again. I wasn't as useful to the world as I am now. I couldn't earn a living as easily as I do now. True enough, I could stay up longer hours and get around at night better than I do now, but I don't want to stay up nights now. Of course, with age you lose your teeth but, after all, the dentists can supply you with a set of teeth far better than your own. The expert with a toupee can do the same thing with your hair and, in addition, he can give you any color or texture you want.

Seriously, the worst part of the fear of old age is that it has a tendency to slow you down and causes you to develop a feeling of inferiority just at a time when you are actually in your best years (between 40 and 60). A person should have a positive appreciation for the increased assets of wisdom and understanding that come with more years. Incidentally, that word "understanding" is one of the most meaningful words in our language. It is surely what the world needs most.

Perhaps you are getting along to the point in life where you need a technique for keeping yourself sold on the idea of being able to maintain a youthful outlook. I find that early in the morning, when I first get out of bed, sometimes that old, long-whiskered fellow, Father Time, sneaks up alongside of me and tries to whisper in my ear, "Boy, I'm getting you; you're almost mine." The moment I see him coming, I yell in loud, unmistakable tones, "Get out of here, old man, and stay out! I have no need of your services whatever. Get out of here!" Try this and you will see that it is not so ridiculous as it sounds at first. It is just a technique to get a positive mental attitude while the body is warming up for the day's activities.

SIXTH BASIC FEAR—FEAR OF THE LOSS OF LIBERTY

This fear was manifest on a worldwide scale just a few years ago when certain influences were deliberately at work destroying the hard-won liberty of the citizens of many nations. In fact, we just missed losing our liberty, which this great nation has so far protected. But the battle is by no means over. Those forces that want to stifle human liberty are not dead, only dormant; and, in fact, organizing themselves for a greater onslaught.

The positive attitude for us in this country of the United States is to be ever vigilant and make the most constructive use of the liberty we now enjoy. Perhaps we need to refresh our memories occasionally as to why this nation makes possible greater freedom than any other, and to re-examine our institutions that were set up as safeguards of these precious rights.

No one needs to be a prophet or possessed of any special perception to see the serious threats to our liberty that are daily gaining ground right in our midst. One of the basic ideas of this philosophy is that the "American Way of Life" is essential to individual achievement on any level above mediocrity. Here, I may suggest, is something worthy of your most serious thinking. We must be on the alert to preserve our liberties, lest some apparently well-meaning group "sell us out." No political implication is made, but just the plain fact that liberty is something dearly bought and is preserved only by constant vigilance.

Every person who seeks success in America owes it to himself to understand and respect the fundamentals of Americanism. Those who ignorantly neglect, or willfully refuse to support, the institutions of America may unconsciously contribute to the downfall of the pillars of democracy, thus cutting the very foundation from under their own opportunities for personal advancement. Obviously, no one may enjoy permanent success if out of harmony with the forces that have provided the opportunity to succeed.

SEVENTH BASIC FEAR—FEAR OF DEATH

The seventh and last of these basic fears is the grandfather of them all. This is really a humdinger of a fear—and it is universal.

The reason for this fear is that for untold centuries of speculation on the most profound questions of "Where did I come from?" and "Where am I going?" mankind has conjured up fearful answers. Eternal punishment with fire has been the dominating concept of religious teaching. It is no wonder, then, that people have a fear of death, based on this idea, because eternity is a long, long time and fire is a terrible thing to contemplate. Then, of course, there is a tendency to fear anything we do not understand. So much for the origin of the fear of death. Now how to overcome this fear.

All I can do is to tell you how I got my "foot on its neck." This is the way I whipped the fear of death: I analyzed what we call life and what we call death by observing the way nature works. I found that there are only a few things in the entire universe that we can recognize and isolate. These are time and space, energy and matter and the thing back of all of them—intelligence.

Those five things are all nature has to work with, and I learned in elementary physics that you can neither create nor destroy energy or matter. You can transform it from one state of being into another, but you cannot destroy it. Life is energy, if it is anything. If you cannot create nor destroy energy or matter, you can't destroy life; and nature doesn't destroy it either. That which we call life, like other forms of energy, may pass through successive changes or transitions, but it cannot be destroyed. Death, or the change we thus so designate, is only a transition.

I finally said to myself: "Death is probably one of two things: either death is just one long eternal sleep"–and I don't know of very many things in this world I enjoy more than sleep–"or else, if it isn't sleep, it's an experience on some plane far better than we have on this earth and, in either event, there is nothing to fear because it's going to come anyway."

When you get around to reasoning like that, you take this fear of death and write it off. You don't discuss it or think about it. I can truthfully tell you I am not any more concerned with death than I am with what I am going to have for breakfast tomorrow morning. I will "go" at one time or another and there is nothing I can do about it; therefore, I would be a simple-minded person if I devoted any of my time to worrying about it.

A RICHER LIFE, FEAR-FREE

In closing this section on the basic fears, I wish now to make some general observations that may give you some clues as to how to make your life richer, and free from fears. Anything you fear will trail you around like a pet dog. The mind attracts to it the counterpart of what it dwells upon. The majority of people go all the way through life fixing their minds on all the things they don't want and getting every one of them.

Wouldn't it be a good idea to refuse to think about the things you don't want and feed your mind with pictures of the things you *do* want, until you start getting them? This is one of the greatest things that you can do with Applied Faith. I know of nothing in your entire life more important to you than learning the art of keeping your mind focused upon the things, the conditions, the circumstances of life which you really want. When your mind has Definiteness of Purpose, you are then in a condition to start having Faith, and when you have Faith, you can call upon the greatest reservoir of Infinite Intelligence and enlist the assistance of that Intelligence in carrying out your wishes.

Have you ever wondered why prayer generally doesn't work? Has it ever occurred to you that there is something wrong in the way you pray? I can tell you that prayer always works, but not the way you want it to. When you go into prayer with your fingers crossed, after everything else has failed, and you only half-way believe you will get your answer, when you approach prayer with such a negative mental attitude, you won't get the answers you want. When the dominating thought in your mind is negative, you may be sure that Infinite Intelligence will give you a negative answer.

I can truthfully tell you that never in my life did I attempt to accomplish an act or achieve a purpose that I failed to complete if I conditioned my mind properly before I started. It all depends on the way you condition your mind. This applies to prayer as well.

All that you need to do to get anything you rightfully should have is to take possession of your mind and use it, and you do not even have to ask anyone for this privilege. It is yours, now! The approach to liberty, freedom, and an abundance of the material things of this life is through your own mind, by the methods I have described in this and other statements of this philosophy. That is the purpose of this philosophy—to explain to you how you may take possession of your own mind and use it intelligently to fulfill all that you desire.

The development of Faith is a matter of realizing the astounding power of the mind as it adapts itself to the inflowing Infinite Intelligence and then directs that power to some constructive definite purpose. The only real mystery about Faith is *why so many fail to make more use of it!*

A one-sentence definition of Faith: Faith is the art of believing by doing.

The "doing" is the secret. Faith exists only so long as it is *used*. Just as you cannot develop a muscular arm by disuse, you cannot develop Faith by merely talking about it or thinking about it. Two words are inseparably associated with Faith—"persistence" and "action." Faith *comes* as a result of putting *persistent action* behind *Definiteness of Purpose*. Strong purpose and a sound motive clear the mind of many doubts and fears and other negatives, which must be removed to permit Faith to operate. When you desire anything and pursue that desire actively, you will soon find your mind opening automatically for the guidance of Faith.

A wise, Faith-filled ancient philosopher said, "Faith without works is dead," which is as true today as then.

Faith without works is dead.

Before the state of mind known as Faith will produce practical results, it must be expressed in some form of action. I would give anything in this world, short of my life, if I could transfer to you my capacity to use Faith. I am trying my best to do just that.

Have you ever had a little garden spot of your own? Have you ever had the experience of raising things? I admire people who dig in the dirt. Oh, I know lots of people who dig and spread "dirt," all right, but that's not the kind I mean. Anyone who has kept a garden knows that it is a continual job to keep out the weeds. Somehow the weeds always seem to grow a little faster than the vegetables. You have to adopt whatever measures you have found effective to fight those weeds, while at the same time you have to water, fertilize, and cultivate the vegetables.

The same thing goes on in your mind. It will grow a rich crop, but you have to keep the soil planted with seeds of what you desire and see that they get plenty of the sunshine of your Faith, to bring them to fruition. You have to keep out the weeds of fear, doubt, discouragement, and thoughts of self-limitation.

The following is a poem that beautifully expresses the thoughts I wish to give you at this moment:

Our prayers are answered; each unspoken thought
And each desire implanted in the mind
Bears its own harvest, after its own kind;
Who dreams of beauty has already caught
The flash of angel wings. Who seeks to find
True wisdom shall assuredly be taught.
But thorns of fate have thorny thoughts behind;
For out of our own hearts our lives are wrought,
Be on thy guard, my soul, lest wind-blown seed
Into the fertile soil of thought should fall
And lodging place within the garden wall
Be given to bitter rue or noxious weed.

Unspoken prayers bear fruitage. Love thoughts call
Forth into being every loving deed.
Idle or earnest, still our prayers are all
Answered according to our inward creed.

QUESTIONS TO CONSIDER...

1. Which one of the seven fears most negatively affects your life because you think about it often? Which one of the seven fears has no adverse effect on your life because it rarely comes to mind?

2. In the self-analysis sections, did you see areas in your life where you can improve? Will you take action to correct the misconceptions you have about needless fears?

3. Do you believe that until you get the fear of poverty out of your consciousness, you will not get ahead in life?

4. The author believes: "Death is probably one of two things: either death is just one long eternal sleep—and I don't know of very many things in this world I enjoy more than sleep—or else, if it isn't sleep, it's an experience on some plane far better than we have on this earth and, in either event, there is nothing to fear because it's going to come anyway." How does this compare to your thoughts about death?

5. Are you growing in your mind the weeds of fear, doubt, discouragement, and thoughts of self-limitation? Or are you growing in your mind the fruits of success, joy, and contentment?

7

A NUCLEAR PHYSICS LESSON

Since man has learned the secrets of the atom, the conclusion is inescapable that the Law of Attraction, which has for centuries been taught by some of the occult mystics and has more recently been revived and taught by the believers in the so-called "New Thought/Age" movement, is the true principle of growth. Everything, animate or inanimate, starts out as a nucleus–a whirling bit of energy which, although so small as to defy the lens of the microscope, has the power to attract to itself whatever of a like nature it requires for its sustenance and growth.

Consider the acorn and a handful of earth. Locked up within that acorn is the germ of life, the nucleus that is capable of drawing from its surrounding elements of soil, air, water, and sunlight, the materials to build an oak tree.

Take a seed of corn or wheat and plant it in the ground, and it will create an orbit, or center of activity that attracts from its environment the precise balance of chemical constituents to produce a cornstalk, or a wheat sheaf, and bring forth reproduction of itself, according to the law of growth and increased returns.

These analogies reveal the true picture of the power of the mind to establish a seed of desire and, through repetition of the desire, feed and nourish it by the stimulus of high emotion, and germinated by the sunshine of our Faith, to attract to itself from out of the bounteous supply of life energy from Infinite Intelligence, the practical plans for it to be brought forth as a physical counterpart of the original seed.

Every seed has, in itself, the potentially perfect plant. Every worthy desire has in it the potential power for its perfect fulfillment. For a seed to germinate and produce a crop after its kind it must be planted in fertile soil, it must have nourishment, and it must have sunshine to ripen it for the harvest. I have often compared the subconscious mind to a fertile garden spot, wherein may be planted the seed of one's creation, which is Definiteness of Purpose, by means of a burning desire that imparts the initial energy unto it and sets up the nucleus around which it enlarges and grows. I have explained how the seed may be nourished and cultivated by persistent action according to one's plans, and through repeated instructions to the subconscious.

In this chapter I further explain how you may attract the vitalizing influence of Infinite Intelligence and focus it on the object of desire. You will soon have the whole process laid bare before you. It is a process going on all around you, in countless forms of life. It is not a matter of theory, it is a demonstrated fact. You have only to adapt it to your purpose.

Professor William James, considered to be one of the greatest American psychologists, had this to say:

If you only care enough for a result, you will almost certainly attain it. If you wish to be rich, you will be rich; if you wish to be learned, you will be learned; if you wish to be good, you will be good. Only you must, then, wish these things, and wish them exclusively, and not wish at the same time a hundred other incompatible things just as strongly.

Bear in mind, I'm not saying you can create something out of nothing. The planting and growing analogy is to impress you once again with the possibility of employing the marvelous powers of your own mind, coupled with and activated by the power of Infinite Intelligence, for the creation of the perfect plan that you can then persistently follow to achieve your major purpose.

TEMPORARY DEFEAT

I am about to make a startling statement, the truth of which you may challenge at first, but I think you will agree with me when you have thought it through: *There is no such thing as defeat or failure, unless and until you finally accept it as such.*

Actually from one viewpoint, there is no such thing as failure, ever. The reasoning behind this statement is that you invariably succeed in bringing to a logical conclusion whatever thought you permit to dominate your mind.

If you harvest a crop of poverty, sickness, inharmony, or neurosis, it is because you have allowed the seeds of these growths to become imbedded in the soil of your subconscious mind and have allowed them to multiply and bring forth after their kind. The law of attraction is operating effectively but, unfortunately, you have turned over the garden to the weeds.

As you can plainly see on the vacant lots in your own neighborhood or in the unplowed fields, every spring there is a tremendous crop of fine, lovely, full-grown weeds. They grow automatically, wherever no one takes the time to dig them up and plant more desirable crops. That's exactly what happens to the average person who drifts aimlessly through life without ever making up their mind about what they want. The weeds take over the soil and keep it busy.

Your motivated mind is never idle; it works all the time. It's up to you to put it to work producing what you want, rather than letting it run wild attracting what you don't want.

I must point out that when you do make up your mind to do something definite, adversities will come along to prevent you from being successful, if they can. They are simply testing your Faith. Your Faith has to be tested a lot to see if you really mean business. When such temporary defeats come, accept them as inspiration for greater effort and determination on your part. Carry on with the belief that you will succeed, because you deserve to succeed.

Be sure you are rendering service equal in value to the riches you seek, and proceed to follow the law of growth and attraction, continue to apply your Faith. Believe that you will receive and it shall be done to you.

Every adversity carries with it the seed of an equivalent benefit!

Faith will give you the power to convert adversities and temporary defeats into an equal force for good. I suggest that you think back over your life and analyze everything that seemed to you to be a defeat. See if you can put your finger on the seed of benefit in each of those circumstances, which enabled you to carry on to ultimate success.

Abraham Lincoln suffered a great loss through the death of his one real sweetheart; but because of that disappointment, the well of the man's heart opened to all humanity and he expressed his love on a nationwide scale, thus becoming the Great Emancipator and our greatest President.

Similarly, the great Charles Dickens was disappointed in love, and he transmuted that tremendous pent-up emotion into masterpieces of world literature.

Thomas A. Edison, accidentally made deaf early in life, chose to turn that handicap into an asset, that enabled him to listen more clearly from "within" and unfold the true genius that benefited the life of all mankind for all time to come.

Former United States President Franklin D. Roosevelt took advantage of the wheelchair confinement, which his physical affliction imposed on him, to cultivate the fine arts of speech and human relations that prepared him for the eminent job of world leadership.

ACHIEVEMENTS THROUGH FAITH BASED ON <u>ACTION</u>

Thomas A. Edison heads the list. He *believed* he could perfect an incandescent electric lamp that would enable man to extend the hours of his productive and recreational activities. Edison met with ten thousand temporary defeats before finding the right substance to make a practical filament to market the lamp.

Signor Marconi *believed* the earth's atmosphere could be made to carry human messages without the use of wires; he carried on in the face of many temporary defeats until he was rewarded by triumph, sparking the radio revolution.

Christopher Columbus *believed* the world was round and that he could find a shorter route to India. Once out on the uncharted ocean, he sailed on and on in the face of threatened mutiny, until he found land.

Madam Schuman-Heink *believed* she would become a great opera singer, although her first teacher told her to go home and sew a fine seam and be contented as a seamstress. Her faith carried her forward to success.

Helen Keller, although deprived of the power of sight, speech, and hearing as an infant, *believed* she could learn to talk. Inspired by a patient teacher, she made an undying name for herself, and she is mentioned everywhere in connection with Faith and courage, persistence and determination, not to mention Definiteness of Purpose.

Henry Ford *believed* he could build a horseless carriage that would give the common man a faster way of traveling from place to place. He withstood the derision of sceptics, lived down the epithet of "crack-pot inventor," and finally sold the world more motor cars than anyone else. The product conceived in his imagination serves mankind in all parts of the globe. He vindicated his Faith in his idea.

The list could go on and on, but you get the point. Study the life of *anybody* who has done *anything,* and you will invariably see Applied Faith in action.

HOW TO DEMONSTRATE THE POWER OF FAITH

Now I give you specific instructions on how to create a Positive Mental Attitude, which is the only way to apply Faith in your life. These steps lead to riches of both mind and spirit, as well as riches of the purse and bank book. They are good mental food. I suggest you adopt them as a steady diet.

First

Adopt a Definite Major Purpose and begin, at once, to attain it. Know what you want and determine what you have to give in return for it. You know by now that there is no such thing as something for nothing. Make up your mind positively what you want from life, then get busy creating something of equal value to give in exchange for it. Plant the seed of your desire and start, right where you stand, to do what you can do to deserve or help its fulfillment.

Be sure that the object of your desire is something you feel you are entitled to. If it is beyond your present abilities, start qualifying yourself, mentally or spiritually or physically, so you will grow up to the stature of the demands you make of yourself.

Remember that Nature is always on the side of right and justice–always harmonize with Nature.

Remember that Nature is always on the side of right and justice—make certain you harmonize with Nature in this respect.

If you have been working hard eight hours a day every day in the week, except Sunday, and with your present abilities have been earning only, say, $60 a week, then it would be foolish for you to suddenly expect to make $500 a week unless and until you prepare yourself to render more and better service than you have in the past. It is all right to aim high and shoot at a mark that will tax your capacity, but if you temper your demands with reason and set goals in steps within the realm of probability, you will be more apt to stick by your Definite Major Purpose than otherwise. Never sell yourself short; but do not set a task for yourself that is utterly unattainable on the face of it.

Second

When you affirm the objects of your desire, through prayer each night and morning, inspire your imagination to see yourself already in possession of them, and act precisely as if you have physical possession of them. The possession first takes place mentally, by imagining it in your mind's eye.

Do you have any idea what it would mean to you right now if you had a million dollars in the bank? Do you know what it would do to your courage? Do you think it would help any? Suppose it remained there the rest of your life and you never touched it. Would it be of any benefit to you? You bet it would! It would give you the courage to go ahead and do the things you wanted to do, and you probably would make all the money you needed from day to day and from year to year, and you would never have to call on that million dollars.

I'll tell you a secret—I operate that way myself. I always keep a certain sum of money on hand in the bank, which I never expect to draw upon, but I keep it there to build up my assurance that any project I undertake will be a success.

Years ago when it took far more courage to try to teach this philosophy than it does now, I carried around on my person five brand-new one hundred dollar bills, just for the purpose of maintaining my own ego. With that backing, which was immediately available should the need arise, I carried on in the face of all problems, with my Faith guiding me and showing me the way. Oftentimes your Faith needs some tangible support, because you're only human, you know. Sometimes the "spirit is willing, but the flesh is weak."

Now I'll tell you a little trick to play on your subconscious mind. It isn't deceiving anyone else, and it is a stratagem that may come in handy sometime. You know, your subconscious mind doesn't challenge what you tell it. It doesn't know when you are telling it the truth and when you are not. So go ahead and tell your subconscious mind you have a million dollars in the bank. If that seems too much, cut it down to half a million. If that's too high, still, make it one hundred thousand dollars, but don't settle for less than that. With the feeling that you have these resources behind you, you will have the courage to go out and put over that deal you're thinking of. It will give you self-assurance to carry you over the hump.

Once you express your desire, you must have perfect Faith in the result. You cannot accomplish anything by expressing a desire and then spending your time fearing and worrying that you will not find the work you seek, not have the money in time to pay your bills, or that some other evil thing will happen to prevent good from coming to you.

Remember the law of attraction. It cannot inspire you with constructive plans and thoughts of defeat at the same time. It must be either positive or negative, and it's up to *you* to decide. After any Definite Major Purpose is clearly held in your mind, the tangible manifestation of plans for achieving it is merely a matter of time and persistent effort.

The law of attraction is either positive or negative— it's up to you to decide to attract success or defeat.

I recall a story I heard of Annie, the tenement girl, who was hired by a fashionable Fifth Avenue New York fashion house to run errands, match samples, and pull basting threads.

Annie loved her job. It was thrilling for her to see the lovely ladies primp before the gold-framed mirrors. She soon became filled with a desire. She began imagining herself as manager of the establishment instead of its lowly employee. Whenever she passed before the mirrors, she smiled at a secret reflection of herself.

Of course, nobody even suspected the secret existence of this make-believe person. She began playing a game, pretending she was *already* the shop owner. Soon the lady patrons began to notice Annie's gracious manners, her careful attention to details.

There was a gradual emergence of this personality. She became Annette, the individual, then Annette, stylist, and finally Madam Annette, renowned costume designer for rich and famous clientele.

Do you recall the story of the Great Stone Face? How the boy in the valley spent his life emulating the ideals that the face inspired in him, and how he saw great soldiers, and merchants, and others come to the town. Each time he expected to see the man who resembled the image on the mountainside. At a meeting one day, he was recognized as the man himself, for he had lived for it. It's a touching and beautiful story. By all means, read it. It's by Nathaniel Hawthorne. And remember this:

> The images we hold steadfastly in our minds over the years are not illusions; they are the patterns by which we are able to mold our destinies.

Third

Associate as many as possible of the nine basic motives with the object of your Definite Major Purpose. Give yourself a strong, compelling motive for doing what you want to do, then renew that motive impulse by bringing it up in your mind frequently during the day. If one of the motives is to accumulate sufficient money to get a fine home, a nice automobile, a well-stocked wardrobe, you should visualize those things around you. Go through the motions of trying on that new suit, or driving that fine car, or sitting in the front room of that house. Do not hesitate to use your imagination to build the fire under your burning desire.

> Build thee more stately mansions, O my soul,
> As the swift season roll!
> Leave thy low-vaulted past!
> Let each new temple, nobler than the last,
> Shut thee from heaven with a dome more vast,
> Till thou at length art free,
> Leaving thine outgrown shell by life's unresting sea.

That poem is from Oliver Wendell Holmes.

Learn how to depend on your Faith. Do not be like the congregation down South where the preacher invited them all to church to pray for rain. When the minister got up, he said, "You're a fine bunch of Christians. Where's your Faith? I asked you all to come and pray for rain and not a one of you brought an umbrella."

Fourth

Write a list of all the advantages of your Definite Major Purpose, and call these into your mind as often as possible. This will make you "success conscious," by the power of self-suggestion. Incidentally, this is one way of feeling really happy, even if your Major Purpose is to get out of the negative environment of your present employment. You can get yourself smiling by thinking of what you'll be doing when you're in a new place you have your eye on. Try this out. I have known it to change a person's mental attitude so completely that he won a promotion almost overnight.

Fifth

Make it a habit to associate with people who are in sympathy with you and your Major Purpose, and get their encouragement. This is one of the most legitimate uses of the Master Mind Alliance. Be careful about taking your relatives into your confidence, as they are notoriously fond of discouraging members of their own family who are trying to grow beyond their former narrow limits.

However, I know of one outstanding insurance salesman whose own wife is his source of encouragement when he hits a slump. Whenever he is out of definite prospects, or the going seems extra tough, he goes home and says, "Alice, I'm off the beam, I can't sell today." That's Alice's cue to get out his previous record of exceptional production and have a talk with him. She sits down and points to the record, and asks, "Whose name is written after that $10,000 policy? Who is that fellow? He's pretty good, isn't he? He sold $30,000 worth that week. I'll bet he could do it again, if he tried. Why don't you go over to the so and so's, they have a new baby."

That's all it takes, that vote of confidence, a slap on the back, the words, "John, you can do it!" Then John grabs his briefcase and away he goes, and he doesn't come back without a deal.

We all need someone to give us a boost sometimes.

Sixth

Let not a single day pass without making at least one definite move toward achieving your Major Purpose. Keep up persistent action! You know when a contractor is building a brick house, he first hauls up the sand and gravel for the foundation, then the bricks, the mortar, the lumber for the scaffolding. Each of these components requires attention and work. Just so, the minor sections of your Major Purpose are comparable to the bricks in the walls of the house. They are laid one at a time, but they add up to a sound structure.

Seventh

Choose some prosperous, self-reliant person who is obviously successful to serve as your pacemaker. Make up your mind not only to catch up with him, but to excel him; but do this silently, without mentioning to anyone what you're doing.

A year or so ago, when I was teaching a class in Long Beach, California, I learned the value of a pacemaker from a very vivid experience. It was one of those terrifically foggy nights, when I could not tell where I was except in relation to the white lines painted on the pavement. The lights of my car did not penetrate very far, so I had to creep along. I managed to catch up to a car however, equipped with fog lights that lit up the white lines for a considerable distance. This extra lighting enabled my pacemaker to travel at near normal speed. I took advantage of his trail breaking and drove along behind him. I knew that if he encountered any obstacles, he would give me sufficient warning so that I could stop and avoid trouble.

So it is in life. If you pick out someone who is traveling somewhat the same road you have chosen, the person will light up the pitfalls for you and you may thereby avoid some of them. Remember to carry your share of the load, however; and when you have passed your first "pacemaker," you assume the role for someone else. One other night when the fog was almost as bad, I led the way for an old car that didn't have sealed-beam lights. I set the pace and he followed through on a trouble-free path.

When selecting a pacemaker, be sure to pick someone who is going the same way you're headed, and make sure that he keeps moving at the speed you wish to travel. If he slows down too much or turns off on a side road, you better switch to another trailblazer.

Eighth

Surround yourself with books, pictures, wall mottos, and other suggestive evidences of self-reliance as it has been expressed by others. Build an atmosphere of achievement and success around yourself. You will see these on the walls of offices of great leaders and in pictures in their homes.

Speaking of the power of mottos, let me tell you what I did at the R.G. LeTourneau Company in Georgia. I spent a year and half there, positivizing their plant and solving their management-labor problems. One of the techniques I used was that of plastering the entire premises with mottos, which were changed frequently. I wrote over 3,600 different mottos while I was there.

For example: "Remember that your only limitation is the one you set up in your own mind." And "Your real boss is the man who walks around under your hat." Keep a scrap book handy and cut out all the clever little sayings that inspire you as you read the daily newspaper or some of the better quality magazines that decorate their pages with them.

Ninth

Adopt the policy of never running away from disagreeable circumstances. Fight with yourself to remove all such circumstances, right where you stand, and right now, before they become inferiority complexes or something worse.

Acquire the habit of looking directly at yourself in the mirror for some of the causes of your disagreeable circumstances. Often it is a characteristic of your own personality, which is at least a contributing factor. Be careful about blaming others until you are sure that you have put your own house completely in order.

Sometimes circumstances are the testing devices that come along to try our mettle, to see what we are made of.

We are what we are and where we are because of the dominating thoughts we have permitted to dwell in our minds. Everyone, like water, seeks their own level.

Give no room to procrastination. If you asked me to name the most disturbing weakness of nine tenths of the people I try to help, I would unhesitatingly say procrastination. It is the one thing that keeps most people from working out a Definite Purpose in life. Trade that word "procrastination" for "Definiteness of Purpose," which is the antidote for this deadly habit.

Tenth

Recognize that everything worth having has a definite price tag on it. The price of self-reliance is eternal vigilance in carrying out these instructions. Your watchword must be *persistence!* Everyone puts things off. This is a trait we must master before we can become self-reliant. Most of us are lazy by nature.

"Do the thing and you shall have the power," said Emerson.

Definiteness of Purpose continuously pursued will cure anyone of laziness!

You will recognize that this chapter is full of meat to chew on and sink your teeth into. It bears repeated reflection until you have the habit of relating yourself harmoniously to the great power available to all of us from Infinite Intelligence. I sign off this chapter with a poem by Ella Wheeler Wilcox:

> You never can tell when you do an act
> Just what the result will be
> But with every deed you are sowing a seed,
> Though the harvest you may not see.
> Each kindly act is an acorn dropped
> In God's productive soil:
> You may not know, but the tree shall grow
> With shelter for those who toil.
> You never can tell what your thought will do
> In bringing you hate or love,
> For thoughts are things and their airy wings
> Are swifter than carrier doves.
> They follow the law of the universe–
> Each thing must create its kind,
> And they speed o'er the track to bring you back
> Whatever went out from your mind.

QUESTIONS TO CONSIDER...

1. *"There is no such thing as defeat or failure, unless and until you finally accept it as such."* Do you believe this statement? If yes, write an expanded version that makes it personal.

2. Re-read Professor William James's statement: "If you only care enough for a result, you will almost certainly attain it. If you wish to be rich, you will be rich; if you wish to be learned, you will be learned; if you wish to be good, you will be good. Only you must, then, wish these things, and wish them exclusively, and not wish at the same time a hundred other incompatible things just as strongly." Write a list of your "hundred other incompatible things" keeping you from attaining what you wish for.

3. Is it true that faith gives you power to convert adversities and temporary defeats into good? Think back over your life and analyze any so-called defeats. Then think about the beneficial results in each of those circumstances that translated into ultimate success.

4. Do you know people, personally or by reputation, who *believed* in their purpose and against all odds achieved their goals? Choose one and do a bit of

research, examining the characteristics that gave them the stamina to succeed.

5. Would your closest friend label you a procrastinator? Your spouse? What keeps you from taking action sooner than later?

8

SELF-DISCIPLINE

In beginning this chapter I outline some definite benefits that a mastery of this Self-Discipline principle will bring to you. And I make some promises: I promise you that if you follow the instructions for using this principle:

1. Your imagination will become more alert.

2. Your enthusiasm will become keener.

3. Your initiative will become more active.

4. Your self-reliance will be greater.

5. The scope of your vision will be widened.

6. Your problems will melt away as snowflakes in the noonday sun.

7. You will look at the world through different eyes.

8. Your personality will become more magnetic, and people will seek you out who had previously ignored or overlooked you.

9. Your hopes and your ambitions will be stronger.

10. Your faith will be more powerful.

That's a pretty good lineup of players for anybody's team, isn't it? The reason I can promise you what I have is because there is no single requirement for individual success as important as self-discipline!

Self-discipline means taking possession of your mind.

You are now learning about the principle that has been referred to as the "bottleneck" through which all of your personal power for success must flow. The word "bottleneck," as used here, indicates a controlled passageway that funnels all the rivulets of power you have been mixing, and blends them into a smooth flowing river of great capacity.

Your mind is the "think tank," vat, or reservoir where you have been creating and accumulating potential power. Now you will learn how to release that power in the precise quantities and in the specific directions that will best accomplish your purposes. Through Self-Discipline, the power you possess becomes condensed and ready for practical application to your daily affairs.

To use a rough analogy, you have been building an automobile to take you from where you are now to where you want to go. You have selected a Definite Major Purpose, based on a compelling motive, which is your "steering gear." You have the "spark" of a burning desire. And now you will learn how to coordinate these units into a smoothly functioning "automobile" with an "engine" of unlimited horsepower.

I think you will agree that when you take possession of your mind and use it, you can set the price tag on your services and make life pay you what you ask. You can see all around you those who fail to do this and who must, therefore, accept whatever life tosses out to them. You can also see that this is seldom more than a bare existence.

Self-Discipline causes you to think first and act afterward.

Self-Discipline begins with the mastery of your thoughts. If you do not control your thoughts, you cannot control your deeds! Therefore in its simplest form, Self-Discipline causes you to think first and act afterward. Nearly everyone does exactly the reverse of this. Most people act first and think later, if and when they think at all.

CONTROL OF EMOTIONS

Self-Discipline gives you complete control over the 14 major emotions, seven of which are positive and seven of which are negative.

Seven positive emotions:

1. Love

2. Sex

3. Hope

4. Faith

5. Enthusiasm

6. Loyalty

7. Desire

Seven negative emotions:

1. Fear

2. Jealousy

3. Hatred

4. Revenge

5. Greed

6. Anger

7. Superstition

You can appreciate the value of being able to eliminate or transmute the seven negative emotions and to exercise the seven positive emotions in whatever manner you desire. The value of emotional control is of increased importance to you as an individual when you realize that most people allow emotion to rule their lives, and that it largely rules the world.

All of these emotions are states of mind, and are therefore subject to your control and direction. You can see instantly how dangerous the seven negative emotions can be if not mastered. The seven positive emotions can be destructive, too, if they are not organized and released under your complete conscious control.

Wrapped up in these 14 emotions is power of a truly explosive nature. If you regulate your emotions properly, you can lift yourself to heights of distinguished achievement. But if you permit your emotions to run rampant, they can dash you to pieces on the rocks of failure. And let me hasten to add that your education, your experience, your native intelligence, or your good intentions cannot alter or modify these possibilities.

A driving motive is the real starting point of all achievement. Everything that you do centers on the major positive motive behind a Definite Major Purpose in life. This motive must be so strong that it forces you to subordinate all your thoughts and efforts to the attainment of that purpose.

Many people become confused between a real motive and a mere wish. Wishing will not bring success. If it did, everyone would be a "howling" success, because all people have wishes. They wish for everything on the earth and even on the moon, but their wishes and daydreams are as nothing until they are fanned into a white hot flame of desire, based upon a definite, compelling motive, and this must become the dominating influence of your mind. It must assume obsessional proportions that will induce action.

SELF-DISCIPLINE IS ADOPTING CONSTRUCTIVE HABITS

What you really are, what you do, either your failures or your successes, are the results of your habits. What a blessing then, that these habits are self-made. They are under your individual control. The most important habits are habits of thought. You will unavoidably and finally display, in your deeds, the nature of your thought habits. When you have gained control over your thought habits, you will be a long way on the road to attaining Self-Discipline.

Definite motives are the beginning of thought habits. You will not find it difficult to keep your mind concentrated on your real motive, once it becomes an obsession. Self-Discipline without definiteness of motive is impossible, and besides, it would be worthless to you. Take the example of some religious practitioners of the Far East who have such perfect Self-Discipline that they can sit all day on sharp spikes driven up through a board. Their Self-Discipline is utterly useless, though, because there is no constructive motive behind it.

Self-Discipline means complete mastery of both your thought habits and your physical habits!

Now I am about to give you one of the most important principles connected with Self-Discipline. It is so important that if you learn it, and nothing more, it will serve you well throughout the remainder of your life and help you to avoid most of the serious situations men and women who lack this key of understanding find themselves facing.

This important fact is that *Self-Discipline calls for balancing the emotions of your heart with the reasoning of your head.* This means that you must learn to consult both your feelings and your reason when reaching a decision concerning each circumstance of your life. Sometimes you will find it necessary to set aside your emotions almost entirely, and follow the dictates of your reason. Other times you will decide in favor of your emotions, but preferably modified by the advice of reason.

Self-Discipline is balancing your heart's emotions with your head's reasonings.

Some men you probably know have so little control over their love emotion that they are like putty in the hands of a woman. I needn't point out that such men never accomplish very much in life. There are, on the other hand, men you know who are cold emotionally, because they follow completely the advice of their heads. This type of man undoubtedly misses many of the finer things in life. The ideal is to achieve and maintain a proper *balance* between these two faculties of the mind—and this is the highest form of Self-Discipline.

Some people have asked me if it would not be safer and wiser to control your life altogether with the reasoning faculty, leaving the emotions out of decisions and plans.

I must answer no to this question. It would be very unwise if it were possible at all. Our emotions provide the driving power, the action force that enables us to put the head decisions into operation. Emotions are the well springs of our greatest power. If you destroyed hope and faith, what would there be to live for? If you killed off enthusiasm, loyalty, and the desire for achievement, you would have nothing left but the faculty of reason—but what good would it be? The head would be there to direct, all right, but it wouldn't have anything to direct!

No, the remedy is control and discipline of the emotions, not elimination. Besides, it is very difficult to eliminate our emotional nature, if not entirely impossible. Our emotions are somewhat like a river. Their power can be dammed up and released under control and direction, but they cannot be eliminated. Through Self-Discipline, we can organize all our emotional power and cause it to flow in a highly concentrated stream in the direction we select, to attain our major objective in life.

So far I have mentioned only the positive emotions. I wish also to call your attention to the fact that the negative emotions can likewise be controlled and transmuted into a constructive

Self-Discipline harnesses and directs our inborn emotions in the direction of our choice!

driving force. Self-Discipline can remove the stingers from these emotions and make them serve a useful purpose. As you know, sometimes fear and anger inspires intense action. But all actions arising from the negative emotional impulses should have the modifying influence of the head so they will be guided aright.

You should submit both the negative and the positive emotions to the examination of the reasoning faculty before letting them loose. This is a major function of Self-Discipline, which maintains a proper balance between the judgment of the head and the sentiments of the heart.

You know yourself that hardly a day passes in anyone's life without "feeling" like doing something our head tells us not to do, if it has a chance.

I want to go a step further and explain another very important idea concerning this balance between the head and the heart. This regards the willpower, or the ego, which I discuss later. Right here I want to say that our willpower should be the final judge of any particular situation or circumstance, and have the final say as to whether the reason or the emotions should be permitted to exert the greater influence.

Self-Discipline should include an arrangement by which the ego, or willpower, may throw its weight on the side of either the emotions or the reasoning faculty and amplify the intensity expressed.

Both the head and the heart need a master, and they may find such a master in willpower. The ego, acting through the will, sits as a presiding judge only for the person who has deliberately trained his or her ego for the job, through Self-Discipline. In the absence of such Self-Discipline, the ego minds its own business and lets the head and the heart fight out their own battles as they please, and often that conflicted mind gets badly hurt.

This very inward conflict that goes on without a referee, causes many people to have problems they are unable to solve for themselves and sends them running to a psychiatrist. This conflict is one of the basic causes of the alarming incidence of neurosis in our culture today. The problem has become more acute as civilization has evolved, because the situations faced by men and women today are so infinitely more complex than those

Emotion without reason is our greatest enemy!

of a generation or so ago. In other words, the need for Self-Discipline is increasing as our culture becomes more complicated in its demands upon the human mind.

The need for Self-Discipline is increasing as our culture becomes more complicated in its demands upon the human mind.

The ignorance of how to proceed causes the average person to neglect developing this conscious control of emotions and reasoning, and allows these two potent forces to literally rend people's minds asunder.

It won't hurt to lighten this up a little by telling a story I heard the other day, which is illustrative of the confusion existing in the minds of people nowadays. It seems that Bill met an longtime friend, John, whom he had not seen for quite a while, and he was bringing his friend up to date on events since their last meeting:

Bill: "I got married since I saw you last."

John: "Oh, that's good."

Bill: "No, it's bad; we're not married now."

John: "Oh, that's bad."

Bill: "No, it's good; you see, she had a lot of money."

John: "Oh, that's good."

Bill: "No, it's bad; she didn't give me any of it."

John: "Oh, that's bad."

Bill: "No, it's good; she used it to build a big house."

John: "Oh, that's good."

Bill: "No, it's bad; the house burned down."

John: "Oh, that's bad."

Bill: "No, it's good; she was in it!"

Well, perhaps that's an exaggeration, but you get the point.

THE BIG THREE

Before leaving this part of our discussion, I wish to point out that not only do we need self-discipline to control emotions, but we need it especially in the case of three other aspects on the "must" list:

1. Mental attitude

2. The use of time

3. Definiteness of Purpose

Mental Attitude

Now about this mental attitude. I have repeatedly stressed in my teachings the importance of a Positive Mental Attitude as the only frame of mind in which you can have Definiteness of Purpose, or by which you could induce anyone else to be motivated to cooperate with you and help you, or by which you could attract the power of Infinite Intelligence in applying your faith.

I feel it necessary, just once more, to remind you that the Creator has given you the right of control over only one thing in all this world—your own mental attitude. You can use it negatively to attract all the things you don't want, or by neglect allow the weeds to take over the garden spot of your mind—or you can pay the price to learn ways to keep your attitude positive and attract what you want in life. A Positive Mental Attitude is the first and the greatest of the 12 riches of life. Without it, it is impossible to enjoy any of the other 11.

Since I mentioned the 12 great riches of life, I want to throw in here the thought that seven of these are directly traceable to Self-Discipline. Look which one heads the list!

1. Positive Mental Attitude

2. Harmony in human relationships

3. Freedom from fear

4. The hope of achievement

5. The capacity for faith

6. An open mind on all subjects

7. Sound physical health

Time

There is an old saying, "Wasting time is sinful." Do you know that the majority of people waste enough time in idle chit-chat to earn for them all the luxuries of life, if this time were more wisely used through an organized time budget? It's sad, but true. I cannot tell you how to spend your time, but I can point out that your time is the most precious asset you have. It's like money in the bank, if it's used correctly. And like money in the bank, it should be spent under the control of strict Self-Discipline.

Time is funny stuff; you can't save it except by spending it with wisdom. The average wage earner works eight hours a day, you need approximately eight hours a day for sleep, and that leaves another eight hours of "free" time to invest as you please. The way this free time is invested makes the difference between success and failure in life. Think this over and resolve that you are going to set up a chart for the expenditure of your allotment of 24 hours.

Definiteness of Purpose

A Definite Major Purpose is the beginning of all achievement, when related to a strongly compelling motive. If you haven't yet made up your mind what it is you want from life, now is the time to act. Write out your chief aim and your plans for attaining it. This is the first step in Self-Discipline. Do you realize that even Infinite Intelligence, as all powerful as It is, cannot help you if you do not make up your own mind what it is you want, and where you are going?

So now we come to the end of this section and I'm sure you see how full of food for thought and action it really is, I have given you a wonderful meal to eat and digest. All of it is positive food for your mind. Now I'm going to tell you about some men who have made astounding demonstrations of the power of Self-Discipline.

EXAMPLES OF SELF-DISCIPLINE

First on the list is one of the most powerful men who ever lived, whose name and picture have been on the front page many times–Mahatma Gandhi. Ordinarily when speaking of a powerful man we think of Henry Ford, John D. Rockefeller, or someone with a lot of money, a lot of property, and a lot of people working for him.

Mr. Gandhi didn't own a house, didn't have any money, didn't even have a pair of pants, and yet he was one of the most powerful men living in this world during his lifetime. That's an astounding statement, until you analyze it and discover the source of his power. Here was a man who over a long period of years, step by step, defeated the great British Empire with all its soldiers and all its other resources. He won freedom for India by using a power the British didn't understand, or chose to ignore. Whatever it was, he must have been dealing with a very great power.

Mr. Gandhi's power consisted of four elements: Heading the list, as usual, is *Definiteness of Purpose*. That's the starting point, and you can easily imagine just how definite Gandhi's purpose was. He knew precisely what he wanted, what his major aim in life was, and he was determined that nothing would defeat him! His was not a selfish purpose. I want you to know that. He was not after anything to benefit himself as an individual. He was planning to benefit the whole of the 400 million people living in India. No wonder he had power. His great motive was unselfish, a burning desire to free his compatriots.

The second factor contributing to Gandhi's great power was the principle of *Going the Extra Mile*. Nobody told him to spend his life as he did. Nobody paid him anything to do it. He was not thinking in terms of a personal payoff. He not only went the Extra Mile, but he went many Extra Million Miles.

You can contrast Mr. Gandhi's unselfish extra service with the kind of selfishness some Americans show. They would have been cashing in on this power for their own benefit, rather than maintaining Gandhi's altruistic viewpoint. Is it any wonder that nothing could stop him in his unselfish devotion to the cause of human liberty?

The third principle Gandhi used in developing this unusual power was *Applied Faith.* You may be sure he cleared his mind 100 percent of all doubt that he would eventually win freedom for his people. He didn't think in terms of fear of the great British Empire. He cared nothing about it, but kept his mind fixed securely on what he wanted. This resolute purpose and persistent action opened his mind to the power of Infinite Intelligence, which is the source of the power of Faith.

The fourth and last source of Mr. Gandhi's power was the power of his own *Self-Discipline.* How do you suppose he kept his mind centered on a Definite Purpose all those years? Don't you suppose he had opportunity after opportunity to capitalize on his situation? Don't you suppose he had temptation after temptation to use his power for his own personal ends? It goes without saying. You and I know that anyone with power is tempted. But Gandhi had the Self-Discipline to live the simple life. He had no intention of accumulating personal property, except a goat or two for milking purposes, and a place to sleep on the floor. I'm not suggesting that you and I should adopt his customs and choose to exist in the simplicity of his personal life, but it is a striking example of the power of Self-Discipline.

THE BANANA PEDDLER

Let's look at another example. We often see a foreigner come to this great country of ours and start out with a basket, just a 25-cent basket, and a handful of fruit, such as bananas. He starts peddling them, and if he sells one, he can eat one during the day. If he doesn't sell one, he can't afford to eat one. By and by, he makes enough to buy a little pushcart. On the cart, he has oranges, grapes, and pears, in addition to the bananas. First thing you know, he has a little hole-in-the-wall store in a shack somewhere, near a parking lot. Next, he leases the lot and builds a building on it. Before you know it, he buys the lot outright and puts up a modern store, which does a thriving business.

The man I am thinking of, Amadeo Giannini, continued to succeed and thrive until he ultimately founded the Bank of America. And all this was possible because he had the Definiteness of Purpose, persistence, Faith, and the Self-Discipline to make what he had fit his needs.

You and I are starting from an improved economic level, and we have the benefit of this philosophy; but we, too, must pay the price tag on success! I want to tell you that wherever you find a person who is succeeding in a big way, you will find a person who has exercised tremendous Self-Discipline.

MY OWN BEGINNING

There were times in my own experience when I didn't have a friend, not even among my relatives, except my stepmother, and I wondered if she wasn't putting on an act. There were times when my opponents said, "He's talking about success and he doesn't have two nickels to rub together himself." And the worst part of it was, they were right!

I put in some 20 years of extreme Self-Discipline. I had to discipline myself to put up with the widespread lack of interest in this philosophy. I had to have sufficient self-interest and Self-Discipline to carry me through those lean years. No matter who you are, when you first start you will encounter almost insurmountable obstacles. I well remember the first class to whom I ever taught this philosophy. It consisted of six people, and four of them walked out on me. One of them refused to pay because he said he didn't feel he had received his money's worth and, confidentially, I think he told the truth.

You have to have Self-Discipline to get over those rough spots in the beginning. You have to discipline your tastes and your standard of living and make them fit what you have right now, until the time comes when you have more.

You will come to the point, sooner or later, when you will want to do something bigger and better than you have ever done before. When you do arrive at that point, you are going to be discouraged by some of those around you who know you best, and who will say the plan you have is foolish or beyond your power to carry out. You will find a lot more people willing to tear you down by discouragement than you will find flattering and building your ego.

The best way to avoid such discouragement is to confide in no one but those who have a genuine sympathy with your cause and an understanding of your possibilities. Otherwise, keep your plans to yourself and let your actions speak. Adopt the motto: "Deeds, not Words." It's a good motto for all of us.

It may not be in the best taste for you to over-shoot your abilities in the way of ambition, but it is a lot better than to under-shoot, and it will do a lot less harm. If you aim at a very big achievement and only attain a moderate achievement, you will still have attained something. If you allow yourself to be held back in the beginning, you have sold yourself short.

Maybe you are a person with a big idea. You have nursed this idea for a long time, You have made an experimental model, or worked it out on paper and refined it over a period of time until you know it will work. But you haven't really done anything about it. The reason you haven't, most likely, is that you lack self-confidence and Self-Discipline.

I want you to take hold of the principles of this philosophy and apply them to yourself. It will do you no good to hear these lectures and think, *Boy, that's a wonderful lesson; I'll bet it will really work for somebody else.* Why not start building up your self-confidence through mastery and application of these time-tested principles that have lifted others from poverty to places of eminence? The rules will work for you as well as for anyone else, but you have to take the initiative; no one else can do it for you.

If and when you present an idea to me for aid in financing it, you may be sure I'll be more interested in you, yourself, than the idea. Anyone with specialized knowledge can detect the validity of an idea, but it is not so easy to detect the qualities of a person.

THAT FATEFUL DAY

Stop for a moment and think about my own story. What a dilemma I was in on that fateful date in 1908 when Andrew Carnegie laid in my lap the opportunity to become the author of this philosophy, based on the experiences of the most successful men in the world. I was only a youngster, barely out of my teens. I didn't know the meaning of the word "philosophy" and there I was with an opportunity like that.

You don't have to use very much imagination to recognize that I had to have a lot of Self-Discipline in order to make myself believe I could do what Mr. Carnegie wanted me to do. And do you know what did the trick? It occurred to me that if Mr. Carnegie, who was the most outstanding industrialist in the United States, thought I could do the job; he must have seen something in me that I didn't see in myself. I banked on his faith in me. Now I'm asking you to bank on your faith in this philosophy and in yourself.

Mr. Carnegie saw in me the quality of "stick-to-it-tive-ness." I didn't have the knowledge of this philosophy myself, but I knew

I could get it from others who did know. He told me that he had turned down 250 other potential writers, because of their lack of "stickability," the quality he recognized in me, although I hadn't recognized it in myself. I have vindicated his judgment. Wise old man that he was, Mr. Carnegie knew that one must possess the determination to stick by a thing and see it through to completion. And he knew that takes a lot of Self-Discipline.

Your success or your failure is entirely a matter of how you discipline your mind.

I have given you some valuable advice. If you grasp and act on what you have been reading, it will be worth more to you than many times the price of this book. You have every quality in the world that it takes to succeed if you will only organize what you have and wrap it up in this philosophy. To do that requires Self-Discipline. You must believe in yourself, and you have to forget about what other people think and concentrate on your objective. Your success or your failure is entirely a matter of how you discipline your mind to create a motivated mindset.

AMERICA'S FIRST AUTOMOBILE DRIVING SCHOOL

I owned and operated the first automobile driving school in the United States and I personally trained more than 5,000 men and women to drive. In the business of teaching people to drive, I have three major rules, all of which call for Self-Discipline.

I have driven all over the United States for many decades and have never had an accident, and I have never been arrested for a violation of traffic rules. That's some kind of a record, I think. I have had a few parking tickets. While I was in Washington on the staff of the President (I served both for President Wilson during World War I, and for President Franklin D. Roosevelt during his first term of office), I had to get to where I needed to be in a hurry, and leave my car wherever I could. I got a few parking tickets for that.

Now here are the three rules:

First

I never, under any circumstances, drive my car faster than will permit me to control the circumstances within the range of my vision, on the right, on the left, behind me, and ahead of me. I keep a sharp lookout all four ways all the time and no matter what the other motorist does, I manage to have my car safely under control. If you don't think it takes Self-Discipline to do this, you just get out on a nice stretch of highway where there is nothing in sight but a lot of intersections, and notice how diffi-cult it is for you to keep your foot off the gas.

Second

I never, under any circumstances, get angry at another motorist or have an argument, even in my own mind, no matter what he or she does wrong. I will tell you why I demand this of myself. The minute you get mad, you don't have control of your car and you have no business on the highway—a car not under control is a lethal weapon. Most people who have accidents are worried or afraid or angry and do not have a positive attitude. Anybody driving without a positive attitude is in danger. The driver doesn't see four ways. He is lucky if he sees one way. It takes Self-Disci-pline not to argue with the other fellow.

I had an experience not long ago that almost caused me to violate this second rule. One of these "Juniors" as I call them, came by me going at a terrific rate of speed. They come up from behind and shoot past without any warning. When this one did that to me, I laid on my horn to let him know I didn't like it. Annie Lou (that's Mrs. Hill) said, "Oh, oh, just a minute; you're going to violate Driving Rule No. 2." I kept my head and whistled a little tune in order not to get mad.

Third

I never, under any circumstances, take an avoidable hazard when I am driving on the road. By a hazard I mean the chance you take when you try to steal a split-second in making a light or trying to run around a curve where you cannot see ahead. It is a hazard to take any chance just to save two or three seconds. In other words, I always feel like the fellow who said he'd rather be five minutes late over here than 20 years early "over there."

I am human enough that I oftentimes feel the desire to save those few seconds, but I exercise my Self-Discipline and refuse to allow this impulse to be carried out by my foot. The average driver in the United States gets that speed rhythm and steps on the gas and takes chances that are really not necessary. In most of our driving, a few minutes one way or the other don't really make a lot of difference. I've often seen someone go whizzing by me on the highway, just burning up the road, only to see that driver sitting idly gossiping with a friend and smoking a cigarette up at the next service station, or other stopping place, with apparently all the time in the world.

These are simple rules, and yet I venture to say that almost all accidents today are due to the violation of one or more of them. I couldn't resist the temptation to pass on these rules for safe driving to you, as an example of Self-Discipline. One reason is that I want my followers to stay alive. Remember, the other motorist doesn't control the situation–you do. If you start using your Self-Discipline, you will help make our highways safer by that much.

RELATIONSHIPS TO OTHERS

Now for a few simple things that demonstrate Self-Discipline in your relationship with others. In my younger days I used to go around not only with a chip on my shoulder, but a whole block of wood and a sign up there that said, "I dare you to knock it off." And darned if somebody didn't always come along and knock it off, too!

As I acquired Self-Discipline, I took down the sign. It helped some, but not enough. I found I had to reduce the block to a chip, which helped some more. Finally, I said to myself, *I will have a shoulder that is fully free, with no chip for anyone to knock off.* I stopped expecting people to find fault, and lo and behold! the world around me began to change from one of disharmony to one of harmony and cooperation. I changed the world I lived in simply by changing my own mental attitude.

At one time I didn't like people who wore loud, flashy clothes. Do you know how I overcame that? I started wearing them myself, to see how I would feel. In other words, by getting the other fellow's viewpoint, I found that under the same circumstances, my reaction was much the same as his.

When you get into that positive frame of mind and quit disliking people just because they're different from you, you will find this a more friendly world in which to live. If you want to get people to see your way or to cooperate with you, you do your part first by getting into the right frame of mind to attract them. You'll be amazed at how quickly they will change their attitude toward you. This matter of Self-Discipline can be made to serve a lot of purposes.

You know, it never does any harm to create a favorable, motivating setting when you are asking someone to do you a favor. Any young man knows the value of a "build-up" when he's courting the girl of his choice. Well, I'm going to tell you something that happened to me where I was the victim of a build-up that almost tricked me into losing a lot of money.

FLATTERY VERSUS SINCERITY

It happened while I was living in Florida. A man flew more than a thousand miles to see me. He started out by telling me how, of all the men in the world, he envied me most, because of my influence and ability to write books and give an inspiring lecture to an audience. You see he was getting close to my heart–touching me in a vital spot. Then he came out with this, "You know, Doctor Hill, you are overlooking a marvelous opportunity and kind of letting Andrew Carnegie down. Instead of retiring and coming down here to play, you should get back into the harness and help cure this world of its sickness. You have the only philosophy to do it." This came as a shock. I must admit that I was believing what he said.

Then he revealed his real purpose for the visit. He had a scheme whereby he would put me on every radio in the country, so that I could sell millions of books instead of thousands. But the catch was that I had to pay him $25,000 in advance to get the thing going. He presented his plan so well, and had touched me in such tender spots, that he had me feeling like I should take him up on his proposition. He had made a careful study of me and realized the proper appeals to make to me.

The one thing that caused me to turn that man down was that he was a stranger to me. That's the only thing that saved me from falling into his hands and parting with my hard-earned cash.

The reason I am telling you this is to show you that it is going to take even more Self-Discipline when you are successful and on top of the heap, and people are complimenting you, than when they are condemning you. Flattery is a tool that has influenced people from the dawn of civilization.

Remember, when anyone approaches you with flattery, he either wants something you have, or he is sincerely appreciative and wants to give you an honest expression of that appreciation. I am grateful that the vast majority of the appreciation I receive is honest and sincere. Only once in a while does someone come along like the one I have told you about. In situations like these, you surely will find good old Self-Discipline handy. It is then when you need to weigh your emotional feelings against your reasoning powers.

The other day as I stepped out onto my front porch, I saw a gentleman standing there. He was a lawyer who had come out from the East somewhere, intending to buy a newspaper here in California. He walked up to me and said, "Doctor Hill, I don't

Self-Discipline helps you weigh your emotional feelings against your reasoning powers.

have an appointment, but took a chance on finding you in with a few moments of time."

I said, "I happen to have a little time right now that isn't occupied." He then explained that he had come to my home to have me autograph a copy of each of my most popular books, *Think and Grow Rich* and *How to Raise Your Own Salary.* While I was writing my name in them, he told me this story:

> I think you would be interested in what these books have done for me. A few years ago, my doctor said I had only a few years to live and he wanted me to get out of my business and go home and do nothing. I didn't want to, of course. He sent me home with *Think and Grow Rich,* and told me to read it, as it would help me. I told him that nothing would help me, but my doctor said, "You're under orders to read that book!" I took it home and started reading. I was reading in bed and I didn't get up until I finished

reading it. That book got me well. That's the reason
I am on your front porch today. I want to be close to
the source—close to the man who wrote that book.

I thanked the man for his great compliment. My pay-off for
the long years I have practiced Self-Discipline comes in just such
ways as that. I had to use a great deal of Self-Discipline to keep
on helping people, back in the times when it was not profitable.
Now that it is profitable, I still practice Self-Discipline to make
sure that I render sincere, helpful service to the students and
clients with whom I counsel. I have to be satisfied in my own
mind beyond a question of a doubt that I have earned my money
before I charge a consultation fee.

I want to tell you that my one policy has always been that if I
got anything in this life, I earned it in advance, making sure that
I didn't overcharge anybody for anything. I must have a policy
of charging people for my time, but there is nothing to hinder
me from waiving a charge sometimes, and I often do, by way of
Going the Extra Mile.

SELF-DISCIPLINE IN MERCHANDISING

I often wonder why merchants are so lacking in principle when it
comes to such a small amount as a half cent. If you buy something
for 25 cents a pound and you only want half a pound, the average
merchant will give you close weight and, in addition, charge you

13 cents. My, my, what an opportunity to make a friend of you, and all for a measly one-half cent!

A great many years ago my stepmother, who was living in the hill country in Virginia, used to order a great many items from Sears, Roebuck and Company. Among other things, I remember on one occasion she ordered a five pound sack of buckwheat flour. When it arrived, she discovered weevils in it and she wrote the company a letter. They asked her to please send it back and they would return her money. When the check came back, it not only included the amount she paid for the flour, but the 12 or 13-cent postage she had put on the package.

I realized afterward that that 13 cents was perhaps the most important 13 cents they ever spent in advertising in that section of the country, because my stepmother became active in the women's club and she told every woman in the county how honest Sears had been. Is it any wonder that Sears, Roebuck & Company was the largest store in the world during that time, doing close to a billion dollars' worth of business a year? No wonder at all, because whoever set the policy in that company realized the value of Self-Discipline and Going the Extra Mile—which is doing what should be done without being told, and then going the extra mile to do much more than expected or demanded to be done. (The numerous benefits of Going the Extra Mile is explained in great detail in *Napoleon Hill's Guide to Achieving Your Goals.*)

QUESTIONS TO CONSIDER...

1. Of the ten definite benefits of Self-Discipline, which one or two appeals the most to you? How would it change your life if this became part of your every day?

2. Of the seven positive emotions listed, which two are you most in tune with and are the most easy to control? Of the seven negative emotions listed, which two are the hardest for you to control?

3. On a scale from 1 (not great) to 10 (really great!) how would you rate yourself when it comes to balancing the emotions of your heart with the reasoning of your head?

4. Have you gone "the extra mile" lately at work? At home? With a person in need? Is it your habit or the exception in your everyday lifestyle?

5. Creating a motivated mind begins with defining your Definite Major Purpose, which is connected to a strongly compelling motive—a burning desire. Not even the all-power Infinite Intelligence can help you if you don't know what you want. If you haven't decided what you want from life, now is the time to act. Write out your chief aim and your plans for attaining it. This is the first step in Self-Discipline, which leads to success.

9

MIND CONTROL

Now I want to tell you some more of the workings of the mind, and especially to describe the rather wonderful machinery for self-government that exists in the mind.

An understanding of the *six departments of the mind that are subject to conscious control* gives you additional information about the principle of Self-Discipline. Please refer to the following chart.

This chart presents diagrammatically everything that is known about the business of thinking. In this chart are shown the six departments of the mind that may be consciously controlled. These six departments will be discussed in detail, as they are the basis of Self-Discipline.

SIX <u>CONTROLLABLE</u> DIVISIONS OF THE MIND

The six divisions or departments of the mind under your control:

CHART OF THE SIX DEPARTMENTS OF THE MIND
Over Which Sel-Discipline Can Be Maintained,
Numbered in Order of Their Relative Importance

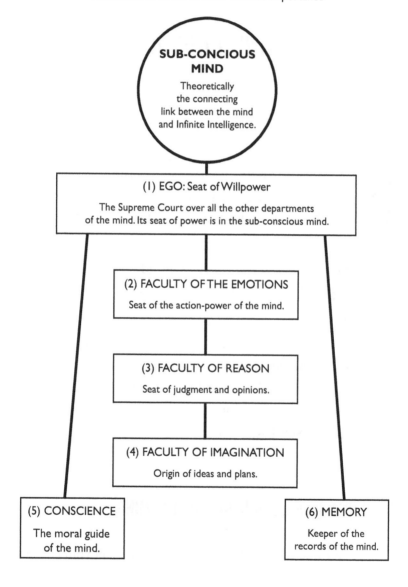

SUB-CONCIOUS MIND

Theoretically
the connecting
link between the mind
and Infinite Intelligence.

(1) EGO: Seat of Willpower

The Supreme Court over all the other departments
of the mind. Its seat of power is in the sub-conscious mind.

(2) FACULTY OF THE EMOTIONS

Seat of the action-power of the mind.

(3) FACULTY OF REASON

Seat of judgment and opinions.

(4) FACULTY OF IMAGINATION

Origin of ideas and plans.

(5) CONSCIENCE

The moral guide
of the mind.

(6) MEMORY

Keeper of the
records of the mind.

1. *Ego.* Ego is the seat of willpower and acts as a "supreme court," with the power to reverse, modify, change or eliminate altogether the entire work of all the other departments of the mind.

2. *Emotion.* Emotion is the driving force that sets our thoughts, plans, and purposes into action.

3. *Reason.* Reason is where we may weigh, estimate, and properly evaluate the products of the imagination and of the emotions.

4. *Imagination.* Imagination is where we may create ideas, plans, and methods of attaining desired ends.

5. *Conscience.* Conscience is where we may test the moral justice of our thoughts, plans, and purposes.

6. *Memory.* Memory serves as the keeper of records of all experiences, and as a filing cabinet for all sense perceptions and the inspirations of Infinite Intelligence.

When these departments of the government of the mind are coordinated and properly guided by Self-Discipline, they enable people to negotiate through life with a minimum of opposition from others.

Self-Discipline is how we coordinate the six departments of our own mental government in such a way that none gets out of control. Self-Discipline thus produces harmony in our mind, which is the reason why I have stressed its importance in this philosophy. You can readily see that Self-Discipline is one principle that every person needs to follow, perhaps more than any other principle of individual success.

After studying this picture of the mind, and realizing the tragedy of neglecting Self-Discipline, many students ask me the logical question: "Why has such a wonderful source of personal power been so generally overlooked?"

In all modesty, I must answer that the main reason is because up to the time Andrew Carnegie commissioned me to organize it, no one in modern times had provided the world with a practical philosophy that incorporated all the essentials of a well-managed life. That great builder of industry and greater maker of men learned, in his dealings with others, of the great need for such a guide as he conceived this philosophy could be. Again, I say, as I have said before, I am grateful and humble in my thankfulness for having been the instrument by which this need has been fulfilled.

Whoever coordinates the six departments of their mind and brings them under Self-Discipline, will find themselves in possession of more power than most people even dream of.

Now for a closer look at the chart:

First–the ego, or seat of willpower.

The ego is the major portion of you that is of value. The rest of you is a collection of chemicals. If scientists ground you up and separated you into those various chemicals, they would bring about a $1.85 at present prices. The part that can't be ground–that represents the ego, which you must learn to control and discipline–may represent anything in value from poverty and ill health on up to anything you can envision as your portion in life. In other words, you set the value on your ego by bringing it under your direction so it doesn't rule you, you rule it.

Now, the ego is a wonderful thing. Some are too weak and too lacking in courage to amount to anything, and some are over inflated. We are all familiar with both types of persons. One is just as bad as the other. There is a halfway point at which you must arrive in the feeding of your ego. Average people, I have found, need to feed their ego and build up courage so they can take possession of their own mind.

To show you how fatal it is to allow your ego to go weak on you, I'll tell you about a man who came to see me the other day. He had been making between $18,000 and $20,000 a year in the ice cream business in the East and then something went wrong. His ego was weakened, so he moved to Los Angeles, where he is now driving a taxicab for $35 a week.

There is nothing wrong with driving a taxicab; it's an honorable business, but it isn't profitable enough for a man who had previously made $18,000 a year. I am going to do what I can to bolster up the ego of this client until he gets back on the beam.

While we're on this subject of feeding your ego, I want to refer to my good friend Edwin C. Barnes, who became Thomas A. Edison's only partner. Barnes "rode the rods" in a railroad freight car over to East Orange, New Jersey, where Edison's laboratory was located, and naturally he presented a sorry sight to the secretary when he asked to see the boss.

You can well imagine how you would feel if you were forced to travel in that dirty, dusty, humiliating style and then, in the same condition, were about to face a successful businessman whom you were interested in impressing. It makes me wince just a little to mention it. Well, Ed Barnes went through that experience and, as a result, you will understand what I'm going to say now.

When the time came that Barnes had vindicated himself and he actually was the partner of the great Edison in the marketing of the dictating machine, he was earning good money, and invested in some good clothes. He always wore the finest imported fabrics, tailored to the height of smartness by the best hand tailor he could find in town. He told me once that he sometimes paid as high as $450 for a single suit, and none that he wore cost less than $250–considerable cost in those days.

And Ed didn't stop there. He had his shirts carefully handmade to order, and his cravats harmonized with his suits. He even had his undergarments made to order, with distinctive monograms on them. This, with handwoven socks from somewhere in Europe, and hand lasted shoes, made up his attire. Nor was this the end. He had 31 such outfits hanging in his wardrobe–a completely new and different suit for each day of the month. He never wore the same suit two days in a month.

When Mr. Barnes explained all this to me, it seemed at first like a show of vanity, but when he told me his reason, I understood what he meant. He said that he didn't dress so finely to impress anybody else; he dressed that way to give assurance and self-confidence to his own ego! He said that the feeling he experienced while standing before Mr. Edison, dressed like a tramp, left such a lasting impression that he resolved ever afterward he wanted to feel that, no matter in whose presence he was, he would be very much better dressed than anyone in the group.

What at first I thought was extravagance I no longer considered as such. I could see his point—he needed to feed his ego that way to overcome the terrible blow it had once received. He was compensating for that injury to his ego.

Your ego is the seat of your willpower, and as such it must be treated so as to remain strong. Whatever that takes, you must include some of your ego stimulator in your daily mental diet. A strong motive never fails. If a motive is deep-seated and desire to attain it is obsessional, it naturally builds willpower.

Before I leave the subject of the ego, I must impress you once again to always treat your ego as your most precious possession. You should protect it as carefully as you would very fine diamonds. You certainly wouldn't leave diamonds around for anyone to pick up, would you? But most people leave their ego wide open for anyone to come in and pollute with thoughts of fear or worry.

Don't let people know your secret thoughts, and do not let other people unload their burdens on you. When your relatives, who are perhaps the worst offenders in this, try to shove off their worries and fears on you, let it all go in one ear and out the other.

You can't even afford to harbor worries of your own, let alone carry around someone else's. You must figure out a technique for protecting your inner self from the damaging effects of negatives.

I want to describe for you the *three walls of outer defense I keep around the ego* I know as Napoleon Hill. Starting with the outside one, and working in, the first wall is just high enough to keep away from me the people who really have no business getting to me to take up my time. This outer wall has several doors in it, and it is not too difficult to enter one of them. If a person can establish a reasonable right to my time, I open one of the doors and let him in, but he has to establish that right.

The next wall is very much taller and there is only one door in it, which I watch closely. The number of persons who get in through that door is comparatively smaller. Before the door swings open to admit anyone, he must have established the fact that he has something I want, or that we have something in common and will be mutually helpful.

The third and final wall is so tall that no person in the world has ever scaled it, and there are no doors in it whatsoever. Not even my own wife is ever allowed inside that wall, because it surrounds and protects the ego of Napoleon Hill. Let me tell you that if you are going to open the door of your ego and personality and let anyone walk in and out, they will take away a lot of what you won't want them to have. I admonish you to throw a protective wall around your mind. Have a place where you can retire to yourself, where you can commune with Infinite Intelligence.

Second-Emotion.

Now we come to the second division of the mind, the faculty of the emotions. Earlier in this book, I had considerable to say about the necessity for balancing the emotions or the feelings of the heart with the faculty of the reason, or the judgments of the head.

Here I want to develop a different aspect of emotions. I want to consider the rather serious problems that arise in a person's mind in connection with disappointments and failures of the past, and the broken hearts that occur as the result of the loss of material things or the loss of friends or loved ones.

Self-Discipline is the only real solution for such problems. The discipline commences with the recognition of the fact that there are only two kinds of problems:

1. Those you can solve.

2. Those you can't solve.

The problems that can be solved should be immediately cleared up by the most practical means available—and those with no solution should be put out of your mind and forgotten.

I want to talk about this forgetting process. I refer to it as "closing the door" on unpleasantness disturbing your emotional equilibrium. Self-Discipline—the mastery over all emotions—enables you to close the door between yourself and the unpleasant experiences of the past. You must close the door tightly and lock it securely, so that there is no possibility of its being opened again. This is the way to treat unsolvable problems, too. Those who lack Self-Discipline often stand in the doorway and look wistfully backward into the past, instead of closing the door and looking forward into the future.

This "door closing" is a valuable technique. It requires the support of a good strong will—you have a strong will if you have organized the departments of your mind and each is under the control of your ego, as they should be.

Door closing does not make you hard or cold and unemotional, but it does require firmness. Self-Discipline cannot permit lurking memories of sad experiences, and it wastes no time worrying over problems with no solution. You cannot yield to the temptation to relive your unhappy memories—doing that will destroy your creative force, undermine your initiative, weaken

Self-Discipline closes the door tightly against all manner of fears, and opens wide the door to hope and faith!

your imagination, disturb your faculty of reason, and generally confuse the departments of your mind.

There can be no compromise with this door-closing business. You must place the power of your will against the door that shuts out the things you need to forget, or you do not acquire Self-Discipline! This is one of the major services Self-Discipline can perform for you. It closes the door tightly against all manner of fears, and opens wide the door to Hope and Faith!

Self-Discipline closes the door tightly against jealousy and opens wide a new door to love! It slams and fastens the door against hatred, revenge, greed, anger, and superstition—your old negative enemies—and stands guard to see that it is not opened by anyone, for any reason.

Self-Discipline looks forward, not backward. It roots out discouragement and worry. It encourages the positive emotions, and keeps out the negative emotions. It not only encourages the positive emotions, but it forces them to come up before the judgment bar of reason each time they express themselves.

Self-Discipline strengthens your mind. It enables you to take possession of your mind and exercise the God-given right to control your own mental attitude. You do not have real Self-Discipline until you can organize your mind and keep it clear of all disturbing influences.

Remember that all the principles of this philosophy must function through your mind, and Self-Discipline, which keeps your mind orderly, is therefore the controlling factor in this whole process of becoming successful. As Andrew Carnegie said: *"The mind is unlimited in its power only to the extent that unlimited demands are made upon it!"*

Third–Reason.

It is not necessary to comment at any length on reason. It is the judge of the "Superior Court" that weighs the creations of the imaginative, modifies the expression of the emotions, and ratifies the decisions of the conscience. This is the portion of the mind trained by observation, study, analysis, and other legitimate avenues of approach to facts and truth. Decisions from this court may be appealed only to the Supreme Court, which is the ego or willpower.

Fourth–Imagination.

The imagination is responsible for all creative effort, as it is the workshop where new ideas are created. It must be carefully controlled by reason and kept within narrow limits. Imagination is an invaluable part of the mind, responsible for all progress in the world. Nothing new or different would ever be conceived if it were not for imagination.

Fifth–the Conscience.

Your conscience is the monitor tucked away in the mind to check on the moral justice of our thoughts and actions. If the conscience is always consulted and its counsel obeyed, it is a valuable component. If it gets neglected or ignored and insulted by a violation of its advice, it often leads to disaster. When this occurs, look out. Society has had to build a lot of special rooms for people who let this happen. The view from these rooms is always obstructed by bars!

Sixth–Memory.

The memory is the filing cabinet of the mind. It is the store house of all the sensory impressions you have ever received by your conscious mind and also every impression that ever reached you through your subconscious mind from Infinite Intelligence. There may be a great many things stored there that never came up to the conscious level, yet can be called forth under certain circumstances by demand from the willpower.

THREE <u>UNCONTROLLABLE</u> DIVISIONS OF THE MIND

There are three elements of the thinking machine that cannot be controlled directly by the individual. You can adapt yourself to them, but you can't discipline them.

One–Infinite Intelligence.

Obviously, you cannot discipline Infinite Intelligence. This is the source of all thought energy, according to the best evidence available. It occupies the mind by the use of Applied Faith.

Two–Subconscious Mind.

This part of the mind is not subject to control by the individual. It is the connecting link between the human conscious mind and Infinite Intelligence, and no one can discipline it. It works in its own way; its major function being that of appropriating and acting upon the dominating thoughts of the conscious mind.

One peculiar characteristic of the subconscious mind is that it will not take orders from the head, or reason. It acts only upon orders of emotions. This is one more reason for acquiring Self-Discipline over the positive emotions, because the subconscious mind will carry out the instructions of the negative emotions just as quickly as it will respond to the positive emotions. It makes no attempt to distinguish between these. The only degree of control you have over the subconscious is by exercising Self-Discipline to impress your conscious mind with your Definite Major Purpose.

Three–Senses.

The five normal senses of seeing, smelling, tasting, hearing and touching. These senses are easily deceived, as for instance in the case of motion pictures, feats of magic when "the hand is quicker than the eye." It is necessary to constantly check the findings of your senses by submitting them to the presiding judge in the court of reason. They are disciplined by voluntary habits.

THE POWER OF YOUR WILL

I cannot close this book without a few special comments on the power of the will, which is seated in the ego itself. This one division of the mind transcends all the others by overwhelming odds. I have already alluded to the willpower as the United States Supreme Court, in comparison with reason, which is the Superior Court, or the next highest court having jurisdiction in the mind. It is almost impossible to exaggerate the importance of your willpower.

As you probably recall from your high school days, teachers of physics always fool new students by asking them what happens when an irresistible force meets an immovable body. Of course, in physics there is no such reality as either of them. However, in the field of metaphysics, there is an irresistible power of force and it is known as the power of the will!

Your only limitation is the one you impose on yourself by limiting the use of your willpower!

Definiteness of Purpose is the starting point of everything you achieve. Willpower, under Self-Discipline, keeps you going until you accomplish your purposes.

The power of the will is irresistible, so it may be said that the only limitation you have is the one you impose upon yourself by limiting the use of your willpower! This is why I have repeatedly warned you against self-imposed limitations.

A person's willpower is so great that it has been known, in countless cases, to restrict even the hand of death. It has performed feats of achievement that have defied description other than as "miracles."

When an obsessional motive is backed by willpower, the subconscious mind has been known to reveal information never before known to man. Thomas A. Edison, Elmer R. Gates, Alexander

Graham Bell, Signor Marconi, and others in the scientific world, solved some of their most perplexing problems in this way.

With determined willpower, you can shut the door on any unwanted memories, and you can open the door of opportunity in any direction of your choice. If you find the first door hard to open, try another and so on, until you find one where you may enter.

The willpower is the Supreme Court of the human mind, and it also sometimes implements and carries out its decisions. There are no short cuts to the control of this mighty power. Yet that control has a price tag, and the price is the understanding and applying of all of the principles of this philosophy, unified and directed by Self-Discipline.

QUESTIONS TO CONSIDER...

1. The six divisions under your control are ego, emotions, reason, imagination, conscience, and memory. Referring back to the beginning of the chapter and the descriptions, which division are you most in control of? Which division are you least in control? What steps can you take to bring all of these division under your control at all times?

2. How often do you "feed" your ego? Would you say you feed it with healthy food, junk food, or do you starve it through low self-esteem and negative thoughts?

3. Imagine for a few moments that you have perfectly coordinated the six departments of your mind and are fully Self-Disciplined—what is the first action you take, knowing you possess more power than you and most people even dream of?

4. Self-Discipline looks forward, roots out discouragement and worry, encourages positive emotions, strengthens your mind, and enables you to exercise your God-given right to control your own mental attitude. Can you profess to have real Self-Discipline in that you have organized your mind and you keep it clear of all disturbing influences?

5. With determined willpower, you can open doors of opportunity in any direction of your choice. What will you set your willpower on today that will open the door to...

ABOUT
NAPOLEON HILL

(1883-1970)

*"Remember that your real wealth can be measured
not by what you have–but by what you are."*

In 1908, during a particularly down time in the U.S. economy and with no money and no work, Napoleon Hill took a job to write success stories about famous men. Although it would not provide much in the way of income, it offered Hill the opportunity to meet and profile the giants of industry and business–the first of whom was the creator of America's steel industry, multimillionaire Andrew Carnegie, who became Hill's mentor.

Carnegie was so impressed by Hill's perceptive mind that following their three-hour interview he invited Hill to spend the weekend at his estate so they could continue the discussion. During the course of the next two days, Carnegie told Hill that he believed any person could achieve greatness if they understood the philosophy of success and the steps required to achieve it. "It's a shame," he said, "that each new generation must find the way to success by trial and error, when the principles are really clear-cut."

Carnegie went on to explain his theory that this knowledge could be gained by interviewing those who had achieved greatness and then compiling the information and research into a comprehensive set of principles. He believed that it would take at least twenty years, and that the result would be "the world's first philosophy of individual achievement." He offered Hill the challenge—for no more compensation than that Carnegie would make the necessary introductions and cover travel expenses.

It took Hill twenty-nine seconds to accept Carnegie's proposal. Carnegie told him afterward that had it taken him more than sixty seconds to make the decision he would have withdrawn the offer, for "a man who cannot reach a decision promptly, once he has all the necessary facts, cannot be depended upon to carry through any decision he may make."

It was through Napoleon Hill's unwavering dedication that his book, *Think and Grow Rich*, was written and more than 80 million copies have been sold.

THANK YOU FOR READING THIS BOOK!

If you found any of the information helpful, please take a few minutes and leave a review on the bookselling platform of your choice.

BONUS GIFT!

Don't forget to sign up to try our newsletter and grab your free personal development ebook here:

soundwisdom.com/classics

ALSO IN THE
LIVE A LIFE THAT MATTERS SERIES:

Path to Purpose
7 Steps to
Living a Life that Matters

Achieving Your Goals
The Four Proven
Principles of Success